SOUTH BY SOUTHWEST

The aim of Zenith Books is to present the history of minority groups in the United States and their participation in the growth and development of the country. Through histories and biographies written by leading historians in collaboration with established writers for young people, Zenith Books will increase the awareness of minority group members of their own heritage and at the same time develop among all people an understanding and appreciation of that heritage.

SOUTH
BY
SOUTHWEST

The Mexican-American and His Heritage

John Tebbel
and
Ramón Eduardo Ruiz, Ph.D.

Illustrated by Earl Thollander

ZENITH BOOKS
DOUBLEDAY & COMPANY, INC.

GARDEN CITY, NEW YORK

1969

DR. JOHN HOPE FRANKLIN, Chairman of the History Department at the University of Chicago, has also taught at Brooklyn College, Fisk University, and Howard University. For the year 1962–63, he was William Pitt Professor of American History and Institutions at Cambridge University in England. He is the author of many books, including *From Slavery to Freedom, The Militant South, Reconstruction After the Civil War,* and *The Emancipation Proclamation.*

SHELLEY UMANS is Director of the Center for Innovation for the Board of Education of the City of New York, a specialist in reading instruction, and a member of the instructional staff of Teachers College, Columbia University. For more than ten years she has been a consultant to many major urban school systems throughout the United States. She is the author of *New Trends in Reading Instruction, Designs for Reading Programs,* and co-author of *Teaching the Disadvantaged.*

JOHN TEBBEL is Professor of Journalism at New York University and a writer for *Saturday Review.* He has written many books, among them *American Indian Wars, From Rags to Riches,* and *Red Runs the River: The Rebellion of Chief Pontiac.*

RAMÓN EDUARDO RUIZ is Professor of History at Smith College and author of three books on Mexico, *The Mexican War: Was It Manifest Destiny?* and *Mexico: The Challenge of Poverty and Illiteracy,* and *An American in Maximilian's Mexico;* and *Cuba: The Making of a Revolution.*

EARL THOLLANDER studied art at the City College of San Francisco and received a B.A. degree from the University of California at Berkeley. As an illustrator of numerous children's books and cookbooks, he has made special trips to various parts of the world to obtain material for his drawings and paintings. Some of the books he has illustrated include *Ramon Makes a Trade, To Catch a Mongoose, The 1000 Recipe Chinese Cookbook,* and the Zenith Book *Passage to the Golden Gate.*

The Zenith Books edition, published simultaneously in
hardbound and paperback volumes, is the first publication
of SOUTH BY SOUTHWEST.
Zenith Books edition: 1969

CONTENTS

Throughout the Southwest the Spanish conquered
the land and set up missions.

PART I

WHO IS THE MEXICAN-AMERICAN?

1. The Imaginary Boundary

Who *is* the Mexican-American?

The easy answer is that he is someone who has come from Mexico to live in the United States, or his parents or his grandparents did so. But like many easy answers, this one is not so simple as it seems. In fact, there is no one word or sentence that would describe all the people living in the United States who may be called "Mexican" or "Mexican-American" because of where they were born or because of the way they look or speak.

"Spanish-speaking" might be a better way to describe them, if all of them spoke Spanish. But not all do. Further, many people speak Spanish who are not "Mexican-Americans"—Puerto Ricans, for example. Then, too, many people who come from Mexico and speak Spanish are really more Indian than Spanish in their origins and their culture. Could the Spanish-speaking minority in the United States be called "Americans from Mexico," then? Yes, because they did not come first from Spain, but were already living in the Southwest before the Anglo-Americans got there.

The problem of trying to find a name that fits is confusing because many of the Spanish-speaking people of the United States Southwest are a racial and cultural blend of Spanish and Indian heritages. They are somewhere halfway between the Indians and the Anglo-Americans. What has always given the Spanish-speakers a sense of unity, however, no matter what they may call themselves, is their sense of separation from, or even opposition to, the "Anglos." They cannot forget that they were there first.

Something both sides often forget is how much a part of Mexico the Spanish-speaking Southwest still is. The more than two-and-a-half million "Mexican-Americans" who live there are matched in the Mexican states just south of the border by nearly an equal number of Mexican citizens. As a result, the boundary between the countries is a purely political one, not taking into account that in every other way it is all one region.

The Spanish explorers first brought the language to the Southwest. Between 1528 and 1602 they traveled thousands of miles slowly and painfully over the vast landscape all the way from Galveston to San Diego, from Sonora to Santa Fe, and up the west coast of Mexico to Monterrey. Always seeking gold and silver, and encouraged to look for it by the Indians who were forever telling them that it existed somewhere else so they would leave Indian lands, the Spaniards got as far as San Diego by 1769. Earlier they had colonized Texas and New Mexico, which became the first white colony west of the Mississippi.

These explorers came mostly in search of gold. Behind them were the colonizers. In his book *North from Mexico*, Carey McWilliams tells about such a colonizer, Juan de Oñate of Zacatecas, one of Mexico's four richest men. He traveled northward in 1598 with eighty-three *carretas*, seven thousand head of stock and four hundred soldiers, planning to colonize New Mexico. Oñate, who was probably the first colonizer, came first to El Paso, then followed the Río Grande to a place near Santa Fe. His followers dealt ruthlessly and selfishly with the Pueblo Indians they found living there. And although by 1630 they founded about twenty-five missions and several settlements, everything they had accomplished was destroyed fifty years later when the Pueblos turned on them. In three days they killed four hundred settlers and drove the rest out of New Mexico. Twelve years went by before Diego de Vargas returned to New Mexico with more settlers. He made peace with the Indians and set up settlements, which are the towns and villages of that state today.

Southern Arizona was first settled by a Jesuit priest. Father Eusebio Francisco Kino is often called "the padre on horseback" because of his fifty journeys of exploration in that region.

Juan Bautista de Anza, another Spaniard, also made a famous journey in 1775. While the colonists of North America's East Coast were demanding their independence, Anza marched from Tubac, Arizona, over the California desert to San Gabriel, and in the following year led another expedition from Tubac to Southern California and on up to Monterey and San Francisco. His second journey has been called "the longest overland migration of a colony in North American history before the settlement of Oregon."

Spreading out in this manner, led by pioneer priests like Father Junípero Serra, the Spaniards established twenty-one missions up and down California, from San Diego to San Francisco. They founded the towns of San Diego, Santa Barbara, Monterey, and San Francisco, besides the pueblos of San Jose and Los Angeles. They set up twenty-five more missions in Texas, but their only lasting settlements there were San Antonio and Goliad (La Bahía), and Nacogdoches. In the end, they had a large and going colony in New Mexico, a string of missions along the coast of California, and some dangerous outposts in Texas and Arizona.

But later settlers who came to southwestern and California towns were not Spaniards, but Mexicans of mixed blood. In Los Angeles, for example, of the city's first settlers, only two were Spaniards. One was a mestizo (of Indian and Spanish blood), two were Negroes, eight others mulattoes, and nine were Indians. The fact is that no more than 0.3 per cent of the entire United States population has been Spanish-born; half of these lived in the states only a short time, and most never lived in the Southwest. The heritage of the Southwest and of California, then, is Mexican-Indian, not Spanish.

Today most of the Spanish-speaking people in the United States live in a broad belt about a hundred and fifty miles wide, which runs parallel with the U.S.-Mexican border from Los Angeles to the Gulf of Mexico. Spanish-speaking people live elsewhere, of course. In Michigan, for instance, sugar companies brought Mexicans north to work in the sugar-beet fields. Their introduction to the United States was a sad one. Transported in boxcars, like cattle, they found themselves unloaded in a strange, cold land and housed in shanties on wheels. During the season they worked from sunrise to sunset in the fields for low wages. In the winter they huddled in shanty colonies, fighting cold and disease, miserable until spring came again. But they survived and some struggled to send their children to schools much better than they would have known at home. These children, and *their* children, often grew up to take a proper role in the life of the community, as full citizens.

In the cities of the Southwest and California, Spanish-speaking people had a harder time. They have known what it is to be discriminated against, to live a slum life, to do hard work for poor pay, and to be considered as second-class citizens by their neighbors. Again, they have fought back and endured, and since the Second World War, conditions have slowly improved although there is still much to be done.

It is harder for the Mexican-American who lives anywhere near the border to understand his situation in the United States when he thinks that this line, running two thousand miles between Brownsville, Texas, and San Diego, California, is imaginary. Sometimes only a barbed-wire fence or a river easily crossed separates the two countries. Going back and forth has always been easy. The Anglos and their neighbors have often quarreled, like close relatives who must share the same house, but never has there been a hatred like that which has existed for hundreds of years between some neighboring European nations. The merging of the two cultures in this broad borderland has done more than anything else to keep the two nations united in friendship despite every difficulty.

Probably the oldest and most solid Hispanic settlement in the United States is New Mexico. The towns in that state are among the oldest in the United States —Santa Fe was founded in 1609, the oldest of the capitals—and New Mexico itself is older than any other state except Florida. There are about two hundred and fifty thousand Spanish-speaking people in New Mexico, or approximately 40 per cent of the population. Until 1800, there were more Indians than Spanish-Mexicans in the territory, and when the numbers of these two groups are added today, they surpass in total everyone else in the state.

Because Spain never succeeded in organizing her American colonies into one union or nation, the Spanish-speaking peoples of New Mexico, California, Arizona, and Texas feel no common kinship even though they have the same heritage. Those in California know very little about those in New Mexico, and the New Mexicans have only a vague knowledge of conditions in Arizona and Texas. Some of them have become so closely identified with the "Anglos" that they do not think of themselves as having a Mexican heritage. The Anglos have tended to divide Mexicans into "good" and "bad," depending on their degree of assimilation into the community. Thus, in Texas there has often been bad feeling between the two peoples for many reasons, one being that Texans remember the Alamo without understanding it. Few know that two of the fifty signers of the Texan Declaration of Independence were native Mexicans, and another born in Mexico was that republic's first vice-president.

For most people in the borderlands, there has been a long history of bad feelings on both sides which is only now beginning to be overcome. Since they first came face to face with each other, the Anglos have been "gringos" to the Mexicans and Mexican-Americans, who in turn have been "greasers" to the Anglos. The story of this long conflict is a sorrowful one. There has been much violence and much everyday competition for land, jobs, and power, along with a great deal of bigotry and hatred on both sides. It has been a one-sided struggle, too, since the Anglos have always had more people, more money, and more machines, so that the Mexican-Americans have been virtually a "conquered" people in their own country. Some of them have felt defeated in spirit, if not in fact. The Mexican-American must have the equality he deserves.

He has given much to the heritage of the Southwest and played an important role in its history. For three hundred years after the Spaniards first came, Hispanic peoples set the examples, through patient experimenting, upon which the economy of the region would be based. They laid the foundations for mining, sheep and cattle raising, as well as irrigated farming—all basic elements in the Southwest's present economy.

2. Builders of the Southwest

The Spaniards first came looking for gold and silver. Their Spanish-Mexican-Indian descendants three hundred years later came in search of bread and jobs, in a great wave of migration during the first thirty years of this century. Almost 10 per cent of the population of Mexico moved to the Southwest in that period —more than a million people. They were ready to work at anything—chopping brush, building railroads, working in the copper mines, picking crops, doing any kind of field work. Most of these people settled in the borderlands and played an important role in building the railroads, building the cotton and sugar-beet industries, and making profitable truck or produce farming. The growth of the Southwest as an economic empire was due in no small part to their labor.

Not many laboring men could have lived through what these people suffered in the cotton fields of the San Joaquin Valley, the cantaloupe fields of the Imperial Valley, and the copper mines of Morenci. They withstood the intense heat of the desert and performed the hard, monotonous stoop-labor, hand-labor jobs which were necessary in southwestern agriculture. The owners of these crops and mines could not have done without them, since the Mexicans moved to the north when United States laborers were experiencing such a rapid upward movement in their living and working conditions that the southwestern bosses would not have been able to hire many of them.

The hard, cruel times the Mexican lived through in the Southwest were matched in the sugar-beet fields of Michigan, Minnesota, and Ohio, in the steel mills of Indiana, and in other places where Mexicans traveled to find work. But machines are putting an end to these conditions. They have taken over much of the work. Produce is now crated in the fields, rather than the sheds. One machine can pick the same amount of cotton that once required forty workers. Even the sugar-beet industry has become mechanized in the past thirty years. Still there is conflict between landowners and fruit pickers in the Southwest and between wine producers and their labor force in California.

Before the technological revolution began to occur, the Mexican migrants tried to rebel against their conditions by organizing a trade-union movement in the Southwest and this struggle is still going on. The manner in which the owners of mines and fields have tried to put down this rebellion is a shameful chapter in U.S. history, too little known outside the Southwest. It has led the Mexican-Americans to withdraw into themselves and their own communities a little more. Unquestionably the defeats have been bitter for them. But in a less apparent way, it has also been a defeat for their oppressors.

Not much has been done by the Anglos to improve the lot of Mexican-Americans. Their approach has

always been to deal with the results of the great
migration—delinquency, poor housing, low wages, illiteracy, disease—instead of its causes, and to treat the
"Mexican problem" as though it were like every other
immigration, although the Mexicans were here first.
There is a division, too, in the Mexican minority itself
—the nearly three hundred thousand native-born of
native-born parents, as opposed to the Mexican-born
immigrants. The immigrant may be darker, frankly
Mexican-Indian in his heritage, and often has not
learned to read and speaks little English. The native-
born may boast about his "Spanish" inheritance and
try to gain status with the Anglos by calling himself
"Spanish-Colonial," "Latin-American," "Spanish-Amer-
ican," or "native Californian." To the Anglos, they are
all "Mexicans," immigrant and native-born alike. Some
of the native-born have "passed" into the Anglo's
world; most have not, and many do not wish to do so.

They do not wish it because they do not find it
easy to forget their persecution by the Anglos, particularly in California and especially in Los Angeles,
where in the 1940s Mexican-Americans were the vic-
tims of their own rebellions against discrimination of
every kind. The "zoot suit" riots of that time, set off
by much the same conditions which led to the riots
in U.S. cities of the 1960s, touched off attacks by press
and politicians in several famous cases which left
wounds not yet healed.

At the same time, however, Mexican-Americans were
glad to serve in the Second World War—partly be-

The hard work of the Mexican-Americans helped build the Southwest.

cause a high percentage of the U.S. troops killed or captured by the Japanese at Bataan were Mexican-Americans, members of the 200th and 515th Coast Artillery units of the New Mexico National Guard. They had been sent to the Philippines because they spoke Spanish. Before the war was over, nearly half a million Mexican-Americans were serving in the armed forces. Their record in the war, both in the number of men killed and wounded and their courage in the field, did something to ease the bitter memories of Los Angeles as many Anglos took a second look at their Mexican-American neighbors.

Meanwhile, more than a hundred thousand agricultural workers were brought from Mexico by arrangement with the Mexican government because there were too few workers left to work in the United States during the war. Half the men who harvested sugar beets in the Rocky Mountain states were Mexican. They worked in twenty-one states and brought in crops valued at nearly half a billion dollars. Eighty thousand other Mexicans were brought in to work on the railroads. Working on thirty-two different lines, they held the nation's railroads together through the tremendous strains of the war.

While the agreements with the Mexican government over labor ended in 1947, an illegal traffic in workers has continued. Everyone has heard the word "wetbacks," meaning those who swim the border rivers at night to enter the U.S. Others are smuggled in by truck and airplane.

For those already here legally, whether recently immigrated or native-born and the sons and daughters of the native-born, life is better and their numbers are increasing. In all the Southwest, no other ethnic groups have such a high birth rate as the Spanish-speaking and the Indian peoples, and at the same time, death rates are falling. This means that, as a minority, Mexican-Americans are a solid, growing part of the Anglo-American community, and there is every sign that the two cultures will slowly come together.

For a long time there has been an interchange of languages. Each has borrowed from the other, and on both sides a special kind of speech has developed which might be called "Southwestern."

Our English language spoken in the states owes much to Spanish importation. Such Spanish words as marijuana, sombrero, mesa, sierra, arroyo, cañon, chaparral, mesquite, adobe, ramada, cabaña, hacienda, patio, plaza, coyote, jaguar, serape, machete, mañana are used all the time. Also a long list of Spanish words that have become so thoroughly "naturalized" people have forgotten they were ever Spanish—words like vigilante, filibuster, barbecue, corral, tobacco, vanilla, hammock, tornado, cigar, and banana. "Bonanza" is a favorite television program—another Spanish word. More than two thousand cities and towns in the United States have Spanish names. At least four hundred of them are in California, with two hundred and fifty each in Texas and New Mexico, and more than a hundred in both Colorado and Arizona. Spanish place names can be found all over the West and, in fact, in every state in the Union.

So in spite of the bad feelings between Anglos and the Mexican-Americans in the Southwest, their cultures have been coming together. Before the days of the railroads, when the Southwest was an isolated frontier region, there were many Mexican and American marriages. That ended when the railroads came to the Southwest and it was no longer cut off from the rest of the states. Now, once more, it is not so uncommon, even though many on both sides frown on it. Far more than intermarriage, the conflict today centers on the teaching of the Spanish language in schools.

As it is everywhere in the world, the young people hold the most promise for the resolving of old problems. Young Mexican-Americans are getting the educations so often denied to their fathers and grandfathers, and they are graduating from the schools to go into every walk of life. They can be found in increasing numbers in the universities, the arts, the professions. Soon they will achieve a real self-expression which is certain to have a great influence on the Southwest.

The old lines are breaking down in other ways too. That long border between Mexico and the U.S. has less meaning as trade across it increases. The traffic flows both ways. The United States sends to Mexico our machinery, steel, farm implements, and plumbing fixtures; the Mexicans send back their minerals, fish, guano, tomatoes, and chick-peas. And of course the tourist traffic, heavily weighted on the United States side, increases with every year as more people from the states discover the delights of Mexico. All this cannot help lessening the old tensions between the two cultures in the Southwest.

The Mexican-American teachers, physicians, and social workers of today, and the thousands of young students in the schools of the Southwest and California, can look back on a very proud heritage in this country. It was the labor of their fathers and grandfathers that did so much to develop the far West. The railroads meant the building of the West and they are a monument to the Mexican-American laborers who helped construct them.

Mexican-American influence is everywhere to be seen in the cultural life of the United States not only in the West. The cuisine of Mexico, with its variations introduced by the Spanish-speaking peoples here, is to be found from coast to coast and is growing in popularity. Several dishes—Mexican corn, for example —have become standard items in the American cuisine. Our music is filled with Spanish rhythms; the recent great popularity of Herb Alpert and his Tijuana Brass is a striking example. Some Mexican customs, transported north over the border by those who have come to live in this country, have become our customs.

The cultures may merge and influence each other, but as they do, the Mexican-American will not want to lose sight of his heritage. It is a splendid one. He can be proud of it.

The Mayas built over a hundred cities which traded with each other and with tribes beyond their territory.

PART II

MEXICO IS BORN

3. Aztec Ancestors

Into that long and narrow strip of land connecting North and South America—a belt running twenty-five hundred miles from north to south but only from fifty to a thousand miles east and west—there came, about the time of Columbus, a stream of invaders from across the Atlantic. They found living there different Indian tribes who had come thousands of years before from Asia. They had come by way of the Bering Strait, between what is now Alaska and Russia, and had spread themselves over both the Americas. When these two great streams of human migration met and mingled, the story of Mexico and of Latin America began.

The European explorers who later conquered these people called them Indians, thinking they had discovered India. The tribes themselves had their own names. The Totonacs lived on the shores of the Gulf of Mexico; the Mixtecs and Zapotecs made their home in the wild mountains of Oaxaca; the Tarascans fished in the lakes of Michoacán; and the Mayas had their villages beyond the mountains, in Chiapas and Yucatán. The largest, most powerful, and most advanced of the tribes were the Nahuas. They lived in the

Valley of Anáhuac but had conquered all the land around them. One of these Nahua tribes led them all. It was the Aztecs, or Medicans, who lived in their beautiful city of Tenochtitlán. They had built the city on an island in a lake, commanding the rich central part of the Valley of Anáhuac.

Except for the Nahuas, most of the northern tribes in what would later be Mexico were nomads who wandered over the mountains and across the deserts, sleeping in skin tents, eating cactus leaves, the raw flesh of animals, and sometimes each other. The southern tribesmen were much greater in number and more civilized. They were farmers and their civilization was equal to that of the ancient Egyptians. They worshiped tribal gods and built many temples to them.

All these differing tribes had one thing in common, and that was the way they looked. They generally had brown skin, broad cheekbones, straight black hair, and, like the Indian tribes of North America, little body hair. They were patient, cheerful, and courteous people who put the welfare of the tribe ahead of their own.

Little is known about the tribes of Mexico before the Spaniards came to conquer them except that, like the peoples of both the Americas, they had lived in this area for twelve or fourteen thousand years as generally peaceful hunters and farmers. Then, about twenty-two hundred years ago the tribes of southern Mexico, who had lived in an agricultural society, began to grow into a society where differences between classes appeared. This came with the development of

No one knows what happened, but in the ninth century it seems some
great natural catastrophe struck the Mayan civilization.

organized religion and differences in what each man owned.

Among the most outstanding of these southern peoples were the Mayas, who lived in the interior highlands and in the hot, tropic jungles of Chiapas, Guatemala, and Yucatán. In the first eight hundred years after Christ's birth, they built more than a hundred cities, which traded with each other and with tribes beyond their territory. They were largely a peaceful people, greatly interested in science and the arts. They invented a calendar, for example, which helped those who grew maize, their main crop. They had better calendars than the Europeans had some seven hundred years later in 1531. They were skilled carvers in stone and wood, and their pottery and textiles were equally far advanced.

No one knows what happened, but in the ninth century it seems some great natural catastrophe struck the Mayan civilization while it was at its peak. Within fifty years, there was no more building of Mayan cities. They may even have been deserted. More than a hundred years passed before the culture began again, this time in Yucatán. They achieved a splendid civilization once more, but in a much more limited way. The jungle quickly grew back over everything that had been built in Chiapas and Guatemala and it covers the ruined temples there today.

A more ordinary disaster eventually ended the Mayan revival in Yucatán. For a long time they lived in peace and prosperity under the co-operative rule

of the three great Mayan cities, Mayapán, Chichén
Itzá, and Uxmal. Then bloody dictators arose who succeeded each other rapidly. Civil wars broke out one
after the other until finally, early in the 1500s, the
whole civilization disappeared, its end hastened by
hurricane and plague. Every year the Mayas had put
up a pillar to record the date; they built the last one
we know of in 1516.

Already, however, another tribe was rising which
would be even greater than the Mayas in the grandeur
of their civilization. This tribe would become the most
powerful and the most bloodthirsty in its passion for
human sacrifices of all the Mexican tribes. These were
the Aztecs, who had begun as outcast wanderers but
built themselves a permanent home about 1325 on two
small islands in the center of Lake Texcoco. This city
they called Tenochtitlán. Slowly they grew in strength
until they had conquered all the peoples of that valley.
They then sent their armies over the mountains to
conquer and rule every tribe within reach, going as
far as five hundred miles southward, to the Isthmus
of Tehuantepec. They demanded all conquered peoples to pay tribute in food and gold, as well as provide
human sacrifices for the Aztec gods.

As the result of all this loot, Tenochtitlán by the end
of the 1400s had grown to be one of the most magnificent and beautiful cities in the known world, not
surpassed by any in Europe. More than a hundred
thousand Aztecs lived there, the rich ones in luxury,
surrounded by the floating gardens that are still

famous. These nobles had fine houses built around patios, with splashing fountains and flower gardens overlooked by roof gardens. The city had a thriving market place, but its most important buildings were forty temples. Enclosed by an eight-foot wall, they clustered around a giant pyramid almost a hundred feet high, covering more than two acres. At the top of the pyramid was the temple of the Aztec's chief god, Huitzilopochtli. When the Aztecs dedicated it in 1478, so legend says, twenty thousand human sacrifices were lined up from the top of the pyramid to its base, then stretching in a grim line out through the city streets. Dozens of red-robed priests took hours to complete this slaughter of human sacrifices.

Like the Mayan civilization before it, the Aztecs also fell in ruins, and almost as quickly. Enemies surrounded the Aztecs near the end of the 1400s. Some tribes, like the Tarascans who lived in Michoacán, and the Nahuas who lived in the highlands of Tlaxcala, had simply refused to be conquered. The fiercely independent Zapotecs had actually defeated an Aztec army, and rival cities were threatening to revolt.

Nevertheless, Aztec rulers found it hard to believe that any tribe or group of tribes, in the land that was later to be Mexico, could bring down a civilization so grand and powerful as theirs. The great city of Tenochtitlán ruled over the Valley of Anáhuac, where fifty towns grew wealthy in the shelter of the mountains. Past those mountains, past the smoking cone of the volcano Popocatepétl, lay deserts and jungles, full

The Aztecs feared nothing human. Only the gods,
they thought, could destroy them.

of other tribes. But the Aztecs feared no one but the gods, who, they thought, could destroy them.

That was why the Aztecs were so open to defeat by the small band of invading Spanish conquerors. The friendly, awestruck natives, who welcomed the Spaniards, thought they were gods riding across the water in their winged ships. They later came to hate these invaders, who kidnaped them and treated them badly. But the first news of the Spanish coming was wonderful and mysterious to those who lived beyond the Caribbean islands, particularly in far-off Mexico.

4. Glory, God, and Gold

The news of the white man's arrival reached the Aztecs soon after 1502, the same year a remarkable chieftain came to power in Tenochtitlán. He was Moctezuma (or Montezuma, as he is called today), a gentle and generous man, yet a proud one too, and more than ordinarily superstitious. He was devoted to dreams, prophecies, magic, and worship of the gods. This made it easy for such a man to believe, when the first reports of the Spaniards reached him, that the bearded, white-faced god, Quetzalcóatl, had returned.

Quetzalcóatl was an ancient god, worshiped by both the Nahuas and the Mayas. He was the god of air and water and the god of Venus, the morning star. He appeared in pictures as a serpent with the plumes of the quetzal bird, native to the highlands of Guatemala and worshiped by the Mayas. At first Quetzalcóatl's priests were against human sacrifice, and those who followed him worshiped with rituals of quiet beauty.

In time, however, the image of Quetzalcóatl changed. New legends grew up around him, and he began to appear more like a man with a white skin and a white beard, who had come from the East to Mexico. When the civilization of the Toltecs, who worshiped Quetzalcóatl, finally collapsed, it was said that the god had sorrowfully left Mexico, returning to his home in the East. But his followers believed that one day he

would come back again and claim the Valley of
Anáhuac, which was rightfully his.

The superstitious Montezuma, when he heard about
the white-skinned Spaniards, thought that day had
come. If so, it meant the end of the Aztec civilization,
for according to his beliefs, Quetzalcóatl would end
the practice of human sacrifice and begin a golden
age. To Montezuma, signs of the god's coming were
everywhere—a three-headed comet in the sky, a great
light on the eastern horizon that lasted for forty days, a
temple destroyed by fire, another struck by lightning, a
flood in Tenochtitlán from a sudden rising of the lake,
the destruction of an Aztec army by falling rocks and
trees, and reports of men fighting in the sky.

Desperately Montezuma sought to prevent the end
of the Aztecs by making a mighty sacrifice to Huitzilopochtli. He offered up thousands of humans to the
god on a great new altar and had his temple covered
with gold and jewels. All the subject peoples, who
found themselves taxed and robbed and killed for the
glorification of the Aztec god, could not help wishing
Montezuma's fears were true and Quetzalcóatl were indeed at hand. For then they hoped the bloody tyranny
of the Aztec ruler might come to an end.

Some of these peoples had already started to revolt,
and a civil war had begun when Montezuma one day
heard the news he had been fearing: the messengers
of Quetzalcóatl had reached nearby Tabasco.

They were the first party of Spaniards to move inland that far. Others had come to Mexico before them.

In 1517, a party seeking new lands had reached Yucatán. Here the Mayan warriors, who had lived through the collapse of that civilization, drove them off and the Spanish went back to Cuba. But they brought back with them enough news of a strange civilization to whet the appetite of the Spanish commander, Diego Velázquez. The next year he sent out another expedition, which sailed along the Mexican coast from Yucatán to Veracruz. There they found a friendlier welcome from the Tabasco Indians. The leader, Juan de Grijalva, heard for the first time from these Indians about the great inland empire of the Aztecs. At the same time, Aztecs were hearing about him from spies who were watching his every move. Grijalva returned to Cuba without trying to explore farther or set up a colony—the mosquitoes and the lack of adequate food were too much for him—but not before Montezuma's spies had had a chance to draw carefully for their ruler pictures of what the Spaniards and their ships looked like. The sails of the ships, like wings, and the white faces of the invaders convinced the Aztec leader that Quetzalcóatl was in fact at hand. When he prayed to his gods to take them away and the Spaniards seemed to respond by sailing off, he could only believe that his prayers had been answered.

In Cuba, however, Velázquez was now more determined than ever to see what this new land was like. He looked about for a leader and settled on a young man named Hernando Cortez (or Cortés), who had come to Cuba as the commander's private secretary. Since then Cortez had acquired a wife, property, and a consuming ambition. He was willing to undertake dangerous jobs but he was arrogant and too independent. Velázquez realized this while he watched Cortez organize the expedition, an expedition for which Velázquez put up two thirds of its cost. Too late, Velázquez tried to take away Cortez' commission, but the young man saw this coming and on the day he was to lose it, he sailed away. For three months he sailed about the Cuban coast, defying Velázquez, picking up more recruits and supplies. By the time he sailed for Yucatán in February 1519, he had gathered together five hundred soldiers, eleven ships, sixteen horses, ten brass guns, and four falconets. In his heart burned a high ambition. He wanted to be a conqueror.

Cortez had his good qualities too. He was, in fact, a man with an extraordinary, contradictory nature. He could be a gambler, an excessively stubborn individual, and a bold one. He was also a shrewd judge who could talk people into doing things for him. He leaned toward conciliation and intrigue rather than physical force. Yet at the same time he would not think twice about crushing someone without pity if he thought it necessary to gain what he wanted. Most of all, perhaps, he was a born leader of men and that was what he needed most to be when he landed at Yucatán with his little army of rude and unruly soldiers whose minds were on getting loot. His first act was to upbraid a lieutenant who seized the Indians' gold and chickens and order them returned: that was no way to pacify the country, he said. Yet he did not hesitate to invade the temples, destroying the idols and setting up the crucifix and a statue of the Virgin Mary in their place. The Indians had never seen a statue of Mary but the cross was familiar: it symbolized their rain god, Tlaloc.

In Tabasco, Cortez found the Indians no longer friendly. Bad words about the Spaniards had spread to them from their Yucatán neighbors. They attacked the invaders in force, but fell back in superstitious awe and fear of the Spaniards' horses. The Indians had never seen a horse before and thought rider and animal were all one fearsome creature.

Having conquered the Tabascans, preaching Christianity to them and taking their women at the same time, Cortez and his men sailed to San Juan de Ulúa, where they met the Aztecs for the first time. At first, Montezuma received Cortez and his men like the gods he thought they were. Perhaps the Spaniards thought there must be something godlike about the Aztecs, too, as they saw the Valley of Anáhuac unfold before them. The lovely lakes and the glimmering white houses of the fifty towns, the towers of Chalco and of Xochimilco rising out of the water, the white stone and cedar woodwork houses of Ixtapalapa nestled among orchards and rose gardens must have seemed unreal. They traveled into the valley along a five-mile-long concrete causeway to the pyramids and gardens and splendid houses of Tenochtitlán itself. They felt that no explorer would ever again look upon such a land of unbelievable enchantment and beauty.

Cortez, fearing nothing, thought he could rule this land himself, with Montezuma as a puppet ruler. And so he did for a time, using his power to gather together a huge amount of gold and treasure—one fifth to be given to the King of Spain, one fifth for himself, and what was left went to his followers. Montezuma was a virtual prisoner, although a willing one, for the most part. He refused only to worship the Spanish gods. But Cortez insisted on stopping the human sacrifices. He smashed the idols of the Aztecs, put up a statue of the Virgin in its place, and had a mass sung in the holiest place of the Aztec faith.

Slowly, and in spite of Montezuma, the Aztecs were being roused to furious rebellion. It came to a climax while Cortez was away with half his army. He was trying to convince a Spanish force on the coast sent by Velázquez to seize him, that they should instead join him and share the Aztec wealth. In this he was successful, but the violent and uncertain lieutenant he had left in command at Tenochtitlán had meanwhile fatally offended the Aztecs. The Indians were holding a religious festival of their own and began to think that the Spaniards who had insulted them should be taken as human sacrifices. The lieutenant to stop this movement ordered his men to massacre several thousands of the worshipers in cold blood.

When Cortez returned with his force of a thousand men, it was too late. A furious battle raged for a week. Montezuma, who said he only wished to die, was forced to go out and beg his people to let the Spaniards leave in peace. But his own people stoned him and in three days he was dead.

Spanish guns and swords mowed down thousands of the Aztecs, but they came on in greater numbers and more terrible anger, besieging the Spaniards in the palace. The Spaniards tried to escape one rainy night, but were surrounded and slaughtered. Only half escaped, including Cortez. While escaping from the valley itself, they fought another battle in which Cortez killed the wounded Aztec commander as he lay in his litter. The retreating Spaniards found safety with the Aztecs' ancient enemies, the Tlaxcalans, and there the determined Cortez regrouped his forces.

Persuading the crews of several Spanish ships that had sailed into Veracruz to join him, he put together a new army of nearly nine hundred men. He began marching back up the Valley of Anáhuac, destroying towns as he went, except for those whose inhabitants he persuaded to join him. Arriving once more at Tenochtitlán, he besieged it for three months. The Aztecs fought back with great courage and resourcefulness. They refused to surrender. Cortez thereupon began to destroy the city street by street, weeping as he did because he thought it "the most beautiful city in the world." Most of the city was in ruins before the end, and when at last the final surrender came, his army burned what remained of the city.

That was the beginning of Cortez' master plan to make Mexico a province of Spain. He went on to conquer most of southern Mexico and began to rebuild

The magnificent cathedrals of Mexico are a blending
of Spanish and Indian culture.

Tenochtitlán, using the Aztecs as slave labor. No doubt he would have done more but the conspiracies of jealous Spaniards at home finally forced him to go back to Spain to defend himself. Though he tried, he never regained power over the Mexican territory he had conquered. Returning to Mexico in 1530, he quarreled with his successors, tried unsuccessfully to set up a colony in Lower California, and eventually returned to Spain where he died, neglected and debt-ridden, in 1547.

Yucatán was the last of the southern Mexican areas to be conquered by the Spaniards. There the descendants of the original Mayans defended themselves so stubbornly and bravely that only quarreling among themselves kept them from victory. The Spaniards conquered them by brute force and reduced those who survived to slavery. But they never really conquered the people, who refused to learn Spanish and were still fighting the white conquerors as late as the 1800s. Nor did the conquest of northern Mexico prove to be much easier; it was slow and difficult work. A hundred years passed from the time of Columbus' discovery till the tide of Spanish conquest finally stopped in what is now New Mexico.

Then began a long period of colonial rule in New Spain. Mexico became the leading civilization in colonial America in spite of the fact that the Spanish governors, often cruel and ruthless, were determined to carry out policies that were planned to prevent independence. A new kind of social system was set up.

The Spanish-born whites sent from Spain became the rulers, and the Mexican-born whites, known as Creoles, were the aristocracy, while the Indians lived lives of poverty and slavery. Eventually another class grew out of the intermarriage of Creoles and Indians called mestizos. Out of these classes and mixtures came the forces which created the nation known today as Mexico.

Meanwhile, the country grew. Grains and fruit crops were developed; horses, cows, sheep, and pigs were brought over from Spain. New industries sprang up in wool, silk, leather, furniture, ironwork, wines, tiles, and blankets. Moorish, Arabic, and Chinese styles (the first two a part of the Spanish heritage) blended with the art of the Indians. Agriculture failed to develop, thereby laying the groundwork for most of Mexico's future troubles. The haciendas, or ranches, were self-sufficient units whose owners took little interest in expanding beyond their needs. The Indian peons who worked their lands became slaves to the owners as they were also to those who owned the mines, which would become the chief Mexican industry.

The Church and its clergy, which gradually came to own great areas of land and so to gain a power that was economic as well as religious, dominated society. The Indians followed the faith without truly becoming Christians. They treated the images of the Church as though they were tribal fetishes.

The clergy did not bring a Catholic culture to Mexico. Its members enjoyed wealth and privilege, but education was virtually suppressed; there were only ten grade schools in the nation at the end of the eighteenth century. The University of Mexico, founded in 1551, was the first university to be created in North America, but what it taught was narrow and barren. Only the Jesuit seminaries provided a real education, and in the seventeenth and eighteenth centuries they produced many notable scholars and scientists, including Carlos Sigüenza y Góngora, one of the greatest mathematicians, astronomers, and archaeologists of his day. Mexico produced the first books printed in North America, but the printing presses turned out only theological tracts.

Mexican artistic genius found almost its sole outlet in painting and architecture, which were used to glorify the church yet, nevertheless, resulted in a blending of Indian and Spanish cultures to produce an age of great buildings and art. The architecture was especially notable and it can be seen today in the magnificent cathedrals of Mexico, some of which equal those in Europe. There is something of the Aztecs and the Mayas in their carvings, color, and design, and something, too, of the European baroque style.

The great age of Mexican architecture came in the first part of the 1700s and ended with the winning of the nation's independence. After that, no more churches were built for a long time and a hundred years passed before Mexican artists were able to develop a new style that was their own. Thus colonial Mexico left its cathedrals as its cultural monument. Its political and social legacy was a social and economic system that carried the seeds of a mighty struggle for independence.

Padre Hidalgo gave his countrymen their battle cry—*Grito de Dolores* —which was "Independence and Death to the Spaniards!"

PART III

MEXICO REVOLTS

5. "Independence and Death to the Spaniards!"

On September 16, all Mexico celebrates Independence Day. On that day in 1810, a brave, humble Spanish priest, Padre Miguel Hidalgo, gave his countrymen their battle cry, the *Grito de Dolores:* "Independence and Death to the Spaniards!" A pitiful "army" of only four Indians first heard that cry, but their numbers grew rapidly as Father Hidalgo led them out of Michoacán province toward the capital, Mexico City.

These poor Indians and mestizos, carrying the first torch of independence, were met and crushed by the Spaniards and Creoles. They executed Father Hidalgo. Then another poor padre, José María Morelos, took up the fight. For three years he led the Mexicans in their struggle against the unequal weight of the Spanish government. They were inspired not only by the examples of the American and French revolutions, but also by their own deep hatred of Spanish rule. But Padre Morelos could not muster enough strength to overthrow the government. Like Hidalgo, his Church

excommunicated him, called him a traitor, and in
1815 had him shot as one. Thus, at the very beginning,
the Church lost its political control of the people, although the people remained faithful in their religious
beliefs. The Church had put herself on the side of
the forces of Spain and oppression, and the people
of Mexico for more than a hundred years afterward
thought of it as a symbol of foreign control.

What Hidalgo and Morelos had begun, other men
lived to complete. For eight years, between 1812 and
1820, revolution wracked Mexico, with killing, looting,
and burning uncontrolled on both sides. In the end, the
revolutionaries won by an act of treason on the part of
a government general, D. Agustín de Iturbide. He suddenly came over to the side of the independence movement, bringing his loyal army with him. It won the war
for the revolutionists. But it also laid the groundwork
for the chaotic years ahead, when success lay with the
strongest generals with the strongest armies, whichever
side they chose to fight on.

Iturbide became the first Emperor of Mexico in
1821 at a terrible cost to the new nation. The fury of
the war for independence had driven out the Spaniards
and, at the same time, it had destroyed all those
citizens who knew how to run a government. Capital,
property, power—all were gone with the governing
class. Everyone had suffered. More than six hundred
thousand people had been killed. Even the bell towers
of Mexico's twelve thousand churches were empty, or
partly empty, their bells having been seized to be

The padres who fought for Mexico's independence
were shot as traitors to Spain.

made into cannons. Whole cities, more than six of them, were utterly wiped out. Hardly a hacienda, palace, town, or village had escaped some damage.

When the revolution ended, with independence won at so awful a cost, Mexico was left with a heritage of violence and disorder which it would take more than a hundred years to end. Power by means of violence: that was to be the rule in Mexico.

From 1821 to 1857, the country was in chaos. The revolution had been fought by the poor against the rich, but after the poor had won, their lot was not improved. Governments came and went in Mexico City—fifty different administrations in all—during that brief period of thirty-six years. Everything was tried, at least six different kinds of government—everything except rule by the people themselves in a democratic society. One rebellion followed another—more than two hundred and fifty of them.

Nearly exhausted by 1857, and desperately in need of reform, Mexico produced a strong man to deal with the situation. His name was Benito Juárez, a full-blooded Zapotec Indian, born in 1806 in Oaxaca. Juárez had a dream. He thought it was possible to build a new Mexico, based on the middle class.

He had some promising material to work with. Since the birth of the independent Mexican nation in 1821, a whole new generation of young men had grown up. They had lived under Spanish rule and were relatively uncorrupted by the many governments the country had known since independence. Politically, they had grown impatient with the centralist government of the moment, which was ruled by an old tyrant, Santa Anna, who crushed without mercy every attempt at reform.

One of these attempts escaped him, however. It was a federalist movement known everywhere simply as "The Reform." The men behind it were Juárez, who was then governor of Oaxaca, and his friend Melchor Ocampo, the governor of Michoacán. Santa Anna exiled them in 1852. Fleeing to New Orleans, they joined other revolutionaries like themselves, and in the city's little French cafés, they began to meet and plot how to overthrow Santa Anna.

Before they had time to form a plan the old tyrant's role was ended. To everybody's astonishment, a small revolt was unexpectedly successful and overthrew Santa Anna. The leader of the revolt, a veteran Indian general named Juan Alvarez, realized that he was a soldier, not a statesman, and had no idea how to run the country. So he called in the federal exiles from New Orleans to help him. Juárez and Ocampo came back in triumph and went to work.

First they gave to Mexico something it badly needed, a new basic law. This was the Constitution of 1857, which became the law of the land and remained so until 1917. It had a Bill of Rights, like the United States Constitution, and laid out a program of reform. Naturally the centralists, who were now out of power, came out against this program. It also made some of the federalists, who called themselves moderates, very angry. They soon attracted so many followers that they were powerful enough to overthrow Juárez. Juárez fled to Veracruz and set up his government there. Mexico now had two governments, which made another civil war inevitable.

For three years the struggle went on. The United States helped Juárez. England, together with most of the western European nations, supported the moderates. Juárez helped himself by taking over Church property, and in the process brought the Church itself under control of the government. Religious orders were done away with.

In the end, Juárez proved the stronger force. He came back to Mexico City triumphantly in 1861, and once more the Constitution of 1857 became the law. But the moderates were not ready to give up. They turned to their European allies for more tangible support than arms and money, and three great countries responded: Britain, France, and Spain. All three had the same motive for coming to the rescue. They wanted to collect debts which were long overdue. Juárez had stopped payments on them.

An army made up of soldiers from the three nations landed at Veracruz in 1861, but they were no sooner ashore than they began to fight among themselves. It turned out that France wanted something more than the collection of debts. Her ruler, Napoleon III, planned to annex Mexico and make it part of his empire. Since they had no taste for such conquest, England and Spain withdrew their troops and the French marched on alone toward Mexico City, where

Juárez met and defeated them soundly. That was an offense to French honor which the government at home could not put up with. More troops were sent, and the French captured the capital. Juárez and his army withdrew to the mountains of the north, from which they waged a guerrilla war for the next five years.

Meanwhile, Mexican monarchists in Paris had persuaded Napoleon to install an emperor to rule Mexico. The man chosen was an Austrian prince, Maximilian of Hapsburg, married to a beautiful and ambitious woman, Carlotta. A rigged election was held in Mexico, and as a result, the two came to ascend the throne.

To everyone's surprise, Maximilian's sympathies appeared to be with the federalists. This cost him the support of the conservatives and the Church, and at the same time the liberals did not trust him either. Bothered by troubles at home and nervous about the unpopularity of his emperor, Napoleon withdrew military support from Maximilian. Once the French troops had gone, the end of the monarchy was not long in coming. Juárez' guerrilla army captured Mexico City in 1867 and executed Maximilian. Carlotta escaped only because she was in Europe at the time, trying to get more help from Napoleon. When she heard about the collapse of her husband's regime, she went insane, but lived on for sixty years, dying in 1927.

Juárez and "The Reform" were once more in the saddle. Five more years of revolution, however, had left the country in even worse condition than before. There were no banks or railroads; the people were miserably poor. Juárez was not able to carry out many of the promises of his Constitution before he died in 1872. The troubled country and its problems thus fell into the hands of his former comrade-in-arms, Porfirio Díaz. Díaz took over in 1876, after a brief, confused interim rule under President Lerdo de Tejada, during which conditions grew worse every day.

Díaz was able to do what no leader had done before—that is, bring order out of chaos—but once again at a terrible cost. A mestizo, Díaz was something new in Mexican politics. Born in Oaxaca on September 15, 1830, he spoke Spanish, as all mestizos did, and as the Indians did not. The Creoles, of pure Spanish blood, looked down on the mestizos as a lower class.

The son of a blacksmith who died while the boy was still young, Díaz began his life as a carpenter and shoemaker. But his mother saw to it that he got an education in a public school and then a seminary. She wanted him to be a priest, but Díaz was fired by the ideas of The Reform, which he had heard about while still at school. He left the seminary for the Institute of Arts and Sciences, where he became the friend and sympathizer of Juárez. That led him to cast his vote for reform in the election of 1855. When this action became known, he had to flee for his life to the northern mountains, where he joined Juárez' guerrillas. Later, when Juárez returned to power, he became one of the leader's generals and then went into politics as a deputy from his province to the legislature in Mexico City.

No leader could have asked for a more loyal lieutenant than Díaz. But the proud old Indian, Juárez, repaid him badly after the younger man, who as head of a wild guerrilla army, had helped him beat off Maximilian's troops. Díaz was too popular with the masses. When Juárez re-entered the capital triumphantly after the defeat of the French, which Díaz had done so much to accomplish, the leader deliberately snubbed his lieutenant and refused to let him ride in the same carriage. Hurt and angry, Díaz went home to his ranch, where he was a local hero. His followers, however, continued to plot on his behalf. Small army revolts broke out here and there. His friends in congress, who came to be called *Porfiristas,* opposed Juárez every chance they could. And meanwhile Díaz became more and more popular with the people.

Díaz ran against Juárez in the election of 1872 and was narrowly defeated—so narrowly that congress, according to law, had to make the decision as to who won since the President did not have a majority of votes. They chose Juárez, but a spontaneous rebellion against the decision broke out—one that the stern old man put down as ruthlessly as ever. Then he died suddenly of a heart attack and the way was open for Díaz.

For a short time after Juárez' death, the country was ruled by Sebastián Lerdo de Tejada who, as head of the supreme court, was Juárez' legal successor. Díaz did not come to power until November 28, 1876, when a revolution overthrew Lerdo.

That was how this strong, big man with a black, drooping mustache arrived in Mexico City to begin a whole new era in Mexican politics. He faced all the

problems of those who ruled before him. The lives of
people in other nations were being changed at that
moment by great new inventions and advances in
science. But Mexico at this time had only a few miles
of railroad track, not many more of telegraph wires,
and its industries and sanitation were primitive. Poverty
held the people in an iron hand. The United States
economy was exploding after their Civil War and she
was trying to push into Mexico, a move Lerdo had
resisted. Díaz was a good friend of the United States
and he meant to resist no longer.

With a firm hand and a driving purpose, Díaz took
hold of the Mexican economy and government machinery. He forced Mexico City's businessmen to lend
him five hundred thousand pesos at a very low interest
rate in order to finance his government at the beginning. He converted his younger officers and some of
his former bandit soldiery into a kind of mounted police force. He called them *rurales*, and they rode about
the country keeping the peace. They also rounded up
the necessary number of men when forced labor was
needed for government jobs. The rurales became a
cruel but effective police force.

Díaz solved the problem of the middle class by
making them the government's civil servants. They re-
warded him by proving to be neither patriotic nor
trustworthy. Corruption came to be the order of the
day. The government supported the newspapers. Díaz
controlled the whole legal system. He kept the businessmen in hand by taxing them, and the common peo-

ple under control by force, if it proved necessary. Peasants, Indians, and laborers worked without pay on new roads, buildings, and factories. In a move to save the monetary system, the National Bank of Mexico was founded with the aid of a French corporation, and it soon became a powerful government institution.

Even in his personal life, Díaz extended his power. He married an educated, aristocratic girl, Carmen Rubio, the daughter of Senator Manuel Romero Rubio. Carmen not only rubbed off the rough edges from her mestizo husband, but also was soon dealing with the dignitaries of the Church. Scheming, plotting, and intrigue had become, indeed, Mexico's way of life.

On the other hand, and in spite of the methods he used to accomplish it, there is no denying that after 1884 Díaz succeeded in creating a modern economy in Mexico. He planned to make his country great, powerful, and respected. That was why, at any cost, he pushed the building of railroads, the setting up of banks, and the creation of heavy industry. He put the nation's currency on a stable basis and secured its credit abroad. Mexico was prosperous as it had never been before, and at peace. Who could protest that all this had been achieved by the suppression of liberty, which Díaz believed would always lead to anarchy and lawlessness if it was permitted to flourish. He thought an elite government should rule the country in union with private business and called this theory "scientific-ism." His followers, the *científicos,* who promoted it came to regard it almost as a religion. The *científicos* wanted Mexican nationalism to be taught in the schools, and they looked down on Indians and mestizos as inferior people—except Díaz, of course. In their world, the Creoles and other upper classes were to rule.

When the middle-class civil servants discovered that the benefits of "scientificism" were not to be passed on to them, a large crack appeared in the structure Díaz had built. Inflation caused another crack, as wages were held down while prices rose. The aristocratic, rich governors of the states who had their own little empires of concessions, mines, smelters, railroads, and factories were not likely to oppose Díaz, who made their easy life possible. But everybody below the level of the Creoles, who had the best jobs and most of the money, was a potential enemy of the government.

A quarter of the land which the lower classes needed so badly had passed into private hands; the Indians were robbed of what they owned by one means or another. Foreigners owned great tracts of land and, what was worse, the coal and oil beneath the surface. Anyone who wanted land, apparently, could steal it, unless he happened to be a poor Mexican. Among the Indians and mestizos there was bitter poverty.

Díaz was greatly helped after 1895 by a new minister of finance, José Yves Limantour, a slim, pale, little diplomat who worked tirelessly and skillfully behind the scenes. It was Limantour who avoided disaster by carrying out tax reforms and refunding debts, by having the government take over the railroads and put them under one head, and by securing more capital from the United States. Graft, monopoly, and favoritism almost went along naturally with everything Limantour did, on his own behalf and Díaz'. One of Carmen Díaz' friends married Limantour, and soon the finance minister was busy plotting with the dictator's wife.

It could be said that everything progressive being done in Mexico was for a private interest and not for the people—like the railroads, which were built mostly in the north so that the mining and smelting products there could be taken out. But railroads and mines do not feed people. Under the surface prosperity, a time bomb was ticking away. A rich landholding class was strangling the country by degrees, while the standard of living and the buying power of the people remained at a dangerously low level.

This structure, which Díaz had built so painstakingly, collapsed in a great struggle lasting from 1910 to 1917. It was the first social revolution in the history of Latin America. It began at what seemed to be the peak of Díaz' power, when the dictator celebrated both his seventy-eighth birthday and the nation's anniversary of independence. He held a magnificent two-day celebration that rivaled the great days of the Aztecs in sheer splendor. A few months before this celebration, which attracted celebrities from all over the world, Díaz gave an interview to a veteran New York journalist, James Creelman, an old Hearst man. In an unguarded moment, carried away by enthusiasm, Díaz remarked that he could now retire, since the nation was ready for democracy at last.

That was the best possible news for millions of Mexicans who suffered under his dictatorship. Unfortunately, Díaz did not mean it. He meant to run again in 1910 and keep his power, but his casual, politician's words had touched the match to a powder train that blew the nation into seven more years of fierce struggle, ending with the beginnings of fulfillment of all the promises Díaz had made and never intended to keep.

6. Revolution

One of those who read Díaz' words and believed them was Francisco Madero, a young idealist, who looked wildly different from anyone's idea of a revolutionary figure. Less than five feet three inches tall with a high, thin voice, brown-bearded, suffering from a nervous tic, Madero was also a vegetarian and a spiritualist. Born October 30, 1873, in Coahuila, to a Portuguese-Jewish family, his rich parents were far from being revolutionaries. They were wealthy and powerful owners of land, mines and factories, and of a growing wine and liquor business. Naturally, they supported Díaz and Limantour strongly, but Díaz had never trusted this powerful family. He had no reason even to take notice of their eccentric son, Francisco. No doubt he would have thought it the most amusing thing in the world if he had known that a fortunetelling device had said when Francisco was a child that he would one day be President, a prophecy Francisco himself never doubted.

But printed words have unseated more than one ruler, and this was the weapon young Madero had at his disposal. His book, *The Presidential Succession in 1910*, published in 1908, made him a national figure overnight. In it he argued for a free election of a

president. That could be done if Díaz really meant
his retirement. By law when Díaz retired his title would
pass to the vice-president, and these officers had always been hand-picked by presidents. Sometimes they
were real successors; more often they were puppets
whom the retiring President hoped to control and so
remain in power. Madero's book proposed that an uncontrolled election for the presidency should be held
before 1910. Everyone would have a chance, and it
would be the same as electing a new president later
by popular vote. Since it had been foretold so clearly,
Madero believed he would be elected.

As the election approached, and it was obvious
Díaz planned to keep his control of the government
in one way or another, Madero began campaigning
around the country on the idea that even if Díaz were
to be re-elected, the vice-president should be freely
chosen. He would become president when Díaz died,
and the result would be the same.

Díaz tried to ruin Madero's campaign in every way
he could, but the astonishing young man continued
to attract followers. The dictator regarded him with
contempt and fear. Taking no chances, he jailed
Madero a month before the election and tried to put
down his supporters. Some of them were out of reach,
unfortunately for Díaz, and as it proved, these men
were real troublemakers. One was Alvaro Obregón, a
small rancher in Sonora. Another was Emiliano Zapata,
a moody, short-tempered man who was very popular
among the southern peasants.

Díaz was re-elected in July 1910, on schedule, and the result was announced in October, a week after the great centennial celebration. With that announcement Madero, out on bail, decided to escape to the United States where he began organizing the revolution that was to carry him to power. He gained new allies among the unhappy peasantry—men like the rough bandit leader, Pancho Villa, who would become famous in his own right. During the following months, the revolt began in earnest. Rebellions broke out like brush fires. Díaz was like a fireman with only one hose. Nothing could stop the ragged, guerrilla armies. In July 1911, after nine months of fighting, Mexico City fell. Díaz, hanging on to the last, although he was sick and old, got out at the final moment and went by train to Veracruz. From there he sailed for Europe where he was to spend the last four years of his life.

The day Madero arrived in the capital a dawn earthquake toppled buildings, killed several hundred people, and filled the streets with refugees. It seemed to be a symbol of the real revolution that was still to come. For neither was Madero a strong enough man to hold a government together, nor did he understand that Mexico needed social reform even more than it needed political control. The underdogs wanted revenge for everything they had suffered under Díaz.

It seemed that Madero had made up his mind to do all the wrong things. After he was elected President, he told his army to go home and kept the federal army he had defeated. He put Villa in jail for being disobedient, betrayed Zapata, the man who had fought so hard for him during the revolution, and chose a cabinet made up mostly of politicians left over from the old days. These former *Porfiristas* saw that Madero was too weak to govern and plotted to overthrow him. This they did with the help of Victoriano Huerta, general of the federal army and one of Díaz' old strong men, whom Madero had not bothered to remove.

In a frightful purge, which came to be known as the Tragic Ten Days, between February 8 and 18, 1913, Madero was surrounded by his enemies. Huerta had him and the vice-president seized. He was forced to renounce the presidency, then both men were cruelly assassinated. Thus Madero became the first important victim of the revolution he had begun.

In attempting to revenge his death, the new revolutionaries who had followed Madero gave form and shape to the social program that the masses had hoped in vain to get from him. Thus Madero's death marked the outbreak of Mexico's social revolution. In spite of his weaknesses, Madero's idealism and his faith in an honest government of free men left its mark on the events that followed. As a martyr, he died so that others might live in a better world.

One of those who had propelled Madero was Pancho Villa, whose real name was Doroteo Arango. Villa was no statesman. He was a bandit, a guerrilla leader, a general who could hardly be told from his men. Nevertheless this wild, uneducated man had his own influence on the development of the revolution after Madero's death.

The two men could not have been more unlike, although they came from the same part of the country, northern Mexico. Madero was the son of rich land-owners; Villa, a mestizo, came from a poor family of Durango. Born in a small rural village, he began life as a peon working on a hacienda and grew up unable to read or write. On the other hand, he had all the characteristics poor Madero lacked. Self-reliant and daring, he began his real career from the hacienda he worked for and soon became a hunted outlaw, too clever for Díaz' rurales to capture. When Madero's revolution began, Villa joined him eagerly. It was Villa and his men who made possible the major victory at Ciudad Juárez, which broke the back of Díaz' resistance and meant victory for Madero.

There is a story that Villa had urged an immediate attack on Juárez, to which Madero had said yes reluctantly. Then at the last moment he changed his mind. Furious, so the story goes, Villa put his leader in jail long enough to launch the attack that ended in Madero's final triumph, after which the general let his commander in chief out of prison.

Villa's talents on the battlefield were considerable. He had learned the art of guerrilla warfare during his days as an outlaw leader. With his band, he struck here and there, wherever there was loot, employing the hit-and-run tactics that made him famous. Villa was

Villa had complete control of his army and became
the best of the military chieftains.

a natural leader with a strong talent for organization which he showed by his firm control of the unruly army that followed him. He commanded their blind and unswerving loyalty. This included such assassins as Rodolfo Fierro and Tomás Urbina, who liked Villa's policy of asking no quarter and giving none. As the revolution developed, Villa became probably the best of the military chieftains, and his northern division was the most famous of the revolutionary armies.

When Madero jailed Villa after he became President, for his disobedience, the guerrilla leader expected to be shot, and that in fact was the sentence. But Madero decided at the last minute to pardon him on condition that he leave the country. Out of jail, Villa went up to El Paso, Texas, where he stayed until Madero's assassination in February 1913. Villa knew that his real enemies were still in Mexico City and he knew who they were—the old military leaders, chiefly General Huerta, whose false charges had sent him to jail in the first place. Huerta and the others had seen Villa as a threat to their plans for taking over the government, and once he was out of the country, they had a clear path.

But the assassination brought Villa back on the scene, hot for revenge. He raised an army by looting the haciendas of Chihuahua and driving their cattle across the border into Texas, where he sold them to raise the money for guns and ammunition. Two other northern leaders joined him, Venustiano Carranza and Alvaro Obregón. They planned to avenge Madero, carry on the revolution he had begun, and overturn Huerta who by this time had taken over the presidency and brought back the old regime.

With that act, Huerta, without knowing it, had given the revolution a new meaning and purpose. Now it was no longer an act of revenge, but a militant, radical protest against the old order and everything it stood for. It became a movement in behalf of social and economic reform, especially land reform. As a result, it became an agrarian upheaval as well, enlisting the downtrodden peasants in a wide-scale revolt.

Against this force, Huerta managed to hold out until 1914. He was then forced to flee the country, as Díaz had done. In that period of a little more than a year from Madero's death until Huerta's departure, the revolutionaries had fought and won the battles of the revolution, and Villa's army was responsible for many of these victories. From them Villa emerged as the most famous general of the revolution.

If the revolutionaries had only been able to agree among themselves, peace might have followed Huerta's overthrow. Instead, they split up into rival camps. Villa and Zapata led one camp, which had a generally more radical program than the other. Zapata, who was to become the symbol of the revolution, wanted to break up the old estates and redistribute this property among the landless peons. Villa may or may not have had a social and economic program—historians do not agree—but in him the northern small farmers and peasants saw their best hope.

Together, Villa and Zapata opposed Carranza. A somewhat pompous old man, Carranza styled himself the first chief of the constitutionalists, as the forces battling Huerta were called. The first chief had to flee to Veracruz, however, when Zapata and Villa captured Mexico City. He found a valuable ally in Obregón, a military genius who introduced modern tactics of war to the revolution and managed to win the capital back again for Carranza. In the famous battle of Celaya, Obregón defeated Villa and his northern division. He drove him north relentlessly until his army had dwindled away to only a few hundred men. By 1916, Carranza and Obregón had won the day. Villa was thoroughly defeated.

In a desperate and hopelessly misguided gesture, Villa decided to attack Columbus, New Mexico, just over the border. He hoped to draw the United States into the Mexican quarrel by this action, and so topple Carranza, after which he meant to regroup his forces and seize power. But President Woodrow Wilson was outraged by Villa's attack. He sent General John J. Pershing into Mexico in pursuit of Villa—naturally, with the reluctant approval of Carranza, who was willing to approve the invasion of Mexican soil only for that purpose. Pershing, who would soon be commanding the great U.S. expeditionary armies in Europe, was no match for Villa, however, in the guerrilla chieftain's own country. Villa became an even more legendary figure, both in the United States and Mexico, as he led the general on a futile chase through the northern moun-

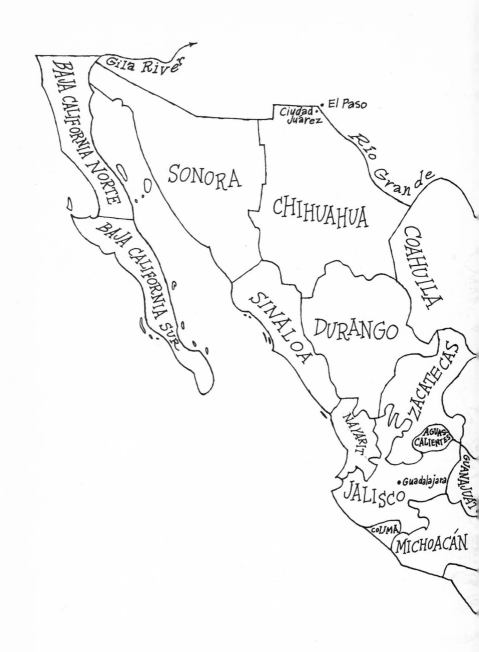

MAP OF MEXICO

San Antonio

NUEVO LEON

TAMAULIPAS

SAN LUIS POTOSI

QUERÉTARO

HIDALGO

MEXICO
Mexico City
TLAXCALA
D.F.
Cuernavaca
MORELOS
MEXICO
Puebla
PUEBLA

VERACRUZ

GUERRERO
Acapulco

Oaxaca
OAXACA

TABASCO

CHIAPAS

CAMPECHE

YUCATÁN
Uxmal
Chichén Itzá

QUINTANA ROO

tains. As a legend, Villa was a tremendous success, but as a revolutionary leader, he had come to the end of the road.

Obregón now took over the leadership of the revolution in a military sense, and when Carranza died in 1920, he became President. Seeking to bring order to the country, Obregón pardoned Villa and gave him a hacienda in Chihuahua, on condition that he behave. Until 1923, the once-feared and fearsome leader lived peacefully on his ranch, raising horses and cattle and doing a little farming. In his lifetime, however, he had made so many enemies that some of them could not let him rest. One night in 1923 he was returning to his hacienda from nearby Parral when his car was ambushed and both Villa and his bodyguard were killed.

Villa had become a legendary figure long before his death, and his sensational departure only added to the legend. Countless books and articles were written about him. Mexican ballads, known as *corridos,* were composed and sung to celebrate his life. For many, he came to represent the romance of the revolution —the Robin Hood who robbed from the rich and gave to the poor. Not much of this was justified, but there was enough truth in it to keep a legend alive. Historians still argue about Villa's merits, but no one denies that he was one of the revolution's great figures.

7. The Underdogs

Zapata was the other side of the Villa coin. Even more than Madero, he was the symbol of the ideals Mexicans died for. And it is his figure that the well-known muralists, José Clemente Orozco and Diego Rivera, painted on the walls of public buildings. Like Madero, Zapata was a man who lived by his ideals and in the end died a martyr to them, betrayed by the same men who were to lead the revolution to its final triumph.

He was a mestizo, more Indian than Spaniard, born and raised in the village of Anenecuilco, in the state of Morelos, just south of Mexico City. It was a tropical state where most of the land served as sugar plantations, with enslaved Indians working the crop. Zapata, a worker like them, rose to be foreman on one of the haciendas. It is said, he first became filled with ideas of the revolution when he saw how much better cared for the horses on the estate were than the men who worked the land and produced the owner's wealth.

Zapata was a revolutionary, and even before Madero came on the scene, he had a small band of men engaged in fighting the plantation owners. It was Zapata's guerrilla army in Morelos, along with Villa's force, which made Madero's victory possible in 1910.

Emiliano Zapata was a man who lived
and died for what he believed.

Unable to read and uneducated though he was, Zapata fought for grand ideals. He made up his mind nothing would stop him from his goal of taking away the land from the hacienda owners and giving it back to the peasants. His ideas on how to do this, which he first presented in 1911, became the basic plan for land reform. The *Plan de Ayala* was put into Article 27 of the Constitution of 1917, which climaxed the revolution. The plan demanded that the lands of the villages be given back to the villagers. Not in the form of individual property, although Zapata saw a need for that, too, but in *ejidos,* an ancient form of land ownership in which the land belonged to the village and was worked in common by its members.

Zapata and his plan became the rallying cry of the underdogs. Both were made famous in the revolution's great novel, Mariano Azuela's *The Underdogs,* which describes the drive of the revolutionaries during their battles against Huerta.

As we have seen, Madero's actions after his victory gave little comfort to Zapata's ideas. Madero said he was willing to adopt them in time, but Zapata was in no mood to wait. And in any case he firmly believed that Madero would never really confront the hacienda owners, since after all they were his own class.

Soon Zapata was in full revolt against Madero's government, and Huerta was sent out to deal with him. The peasant leader was more than a match for the general. After Madero's death, Zapata and Villa joined forces, as described before, to fight Huerta,

and for a time even occupied Mexico City. But Zapata
had no ambition to be President and he went back
to Morelos, leaving politics to Villa.

Carranza's victory did not change matters for
Zapata. The first chieftain accepted the need for land
reform in theory but, like Madero, he thought it could
wait, and in fact had no plans at all to put it into
practice. He accepted Article 27, but did nothing to
carry it out. Zapata, consequently, carried on his war
against the new government, Carranza's, whose troops
had no more success against him than Huerta's. By this
time Zapata had broken the back of the hacienda
system in Morelos and won the loyal following of
the peasant masses. Like Villa, on his own territory
Zapata was unbeatable. He dictated the terms of battle,
and in time he came to control an entire region much
larger than the state of Morelos.

Treachery was the only enemy Zapata could not
conquer. Pretending that he wanted to join the rebel
forces, one of Carranza's lieutenants lured Zapata into
a trap, where he was ambushed and killed in 1919.

Zapata died one of the revolution's most important
figures. He symbolized its idealism, which was really
the battle of brown men, the Indians and mestizos,
for their rights to the land that had been taken from
them. Unlike other revolutionary figures, Zapata made
no attempt to get riches or power for himself. He
never betrayed his ideals or his people. Several times
he refused to accept either haciendas or federal posts

that would have made him a rich man, in return for stopping his struggle, and he died as poor as he had begun.

It is not hard to understand why Zapata ranks highest today among the young idealists and reformers of present-day Mexico. Hated by the rich, he was the hero of the poor—a far more real and admirable Robin Hood than Villa. He took from the rich so that the poor might have more, and that was what the revolution was all about.

The revolution still needed a strong man of another kind to make its ideals come true, and while the generals were struggling with each other and the idealists were failing, one leader was coming up by way of the military to be the nation's political savior.

Lázaro Cárdenas came from the village of Jiquilpan, Michoacán, northwest of Mexico City. His father, a small merchant, saw to it that his son had at least the primary school education. That made Cárdenas an educated man by comparison with most rural Mexicans. He was also the only leader among the revolution's men who came from the small middle class that existed in the time of Díaz, rather than from the peasant masses.

At his doorstep, as a young man, Cárdenas could see the evil that had caused Mexico so much misery. His home town lay in a region where the haciendas had taken over the land of the nearby villages, and his home state, Michoacán, was also the home of the Tarascan Indians. Cárdenas came to know the Indians and to respect them. He read their history and knew how they had been victimized. He did not forget this and to all poor people later he became the most famous champion of their cause in Mexico.

Cárdenas joined Madero's revolution, as might have been expected of a man from this background, and when Madero was assassinated, he helped fight Huerta. As a soldier he was obedient, but not outstanding like Zapata or Villa. Nevertheless, his education and honesty enabled him to rise quickly through the ranks. He became a general while still in his twenties.

The other leaders of the revolution thought of Cárdenas as an obedient servant of the government who could be trusted; as a result, one government after another gave him important posts. He served as military governor of his native state, chief of the army, and head of the National Revolutionary Party, which Calles organized in 1928 to govern the country.

By that time the military phase of the revolution was over. It had ended in 1920, and there followed a period of something like national exhaustion. The country was sick of violence, but its leaders seemed unable to create anything to take its place. The revolution had been won, but none of its promises had yet been realized. First under Carranza, then later under Obregón, and finally under Calles, who ruled either as President or through one of his self-appointed puppets until 1934, Mexico appeared to turn its back on the ideals for which so many men had died. The laws promising land reform were on the books, but nothing had been done to put them into operation. After all the bloodletting, Mexico was still a country where a few rich men owned nearly all the best land.

The depression in the United States, beginning in 1929, struck Mexico with almost equally disastrous effects. There was widespread unemployment and hunger, which only made worse all the old unsolved problems of the revolution. Under Calles, however, the government seemed to have given up any idea of radical solutions. It was only when the continuing pressure of the economic crisis in the early 1930s began to grow worse that Calles saw he would have to do something about meeting popular demands, if it was only a gesture.

In picking a man to succeed him as President, Calles wanted someone he could control, as he had controlled his other puppets, so that he could continue as the real ruler of Mexico. But at the same time he needed someone who could stand as a symbol of reform, to satisfy the masses. He chose Cárdenas, the honest revolutionary and reformer. Cárdenas had encouraged public education and land reform while he was governor of Michoacán, but had always been a loyal supporter of the government. He also had the advantage of being a strong nationalist, which would please the nationalist reformers. Calles and his followers had every reason to believe that by making Cárdenas President they could keep the reformers happy and at the same time they continued to control events themselves.

It was settled then. Cárdenas became the candidate for President in 1934.

So confident of his man was Calles that he failed to take alarm at Cárdenas' behavior during the campaign. There was no question that he would be elected— the well-oiled Calles political machine guaranteed that —yet he went around the country, visiting nearly every village of any importance, listening to the peasants, and hearing their problems and hopes. They seemed to sense in Cárdenas the possibility of their salvation. Soon he found himself the most popular man in Mexico. He was the first candidate in the history of the republic to take his case directly to the people.

Once in office, Cárdenas, the good organization man, shocked Calles by showing to all his independence. He had no intention of becoming a willing tool of the political machine, and quickly showed that he was as much a politician as the old-line leaders. First he worked at winning the army's loyalty, always essential to a President's security. And through his many friends there, particularly among the reform-minded generals, he soon had the military on his side. Then he won over the labor leaders, after which he made peace with the Church, which had been under attack from the state for so long; Calles had openly opposed it.

The most important fact which came out of the new administration was that Cárdenas took seriously the promises made by the Constitution of 1917, particularly those which had to do with land reform. He moved at once to fulfill them. Since Calles had always been

against such reform on a large scale, this led to an
open break between the two men, and Calles threatened to depose his protégé. But Cárdenas, with the
support of the army, the peasants, and labor, was strong
enough to compel Calles to leave the country in 1936.
With him went the conservatives who had been his
supporters. Their jobs were taken by the reformers
who had opposed the Calles machine.

At last, under Cárdenas, the promises of the revolution were going to be carried out. In his first year in
office, 1935, the new President gave back the peasants
more land than all the former revolutionary administrations had done before him. He quickened the pace
of land reform during the next three years, breaking up
the old system and giving the peasants the soil they had
demanded for so long.

Under Cárdenas, Mexico became the first of the
Latin-American nations to support such a program of
land reform. But the President did not stop there. He
had to move rapidly, because he had only six years,
his term of office, to change the pattern of four
hundred years. First he encouraged education, particularly out in the countryside, doing more for them
than any Mexican leader had ever done before. He
built thousands of rural schools, recruited teachers,
trained them, and raised their salaries. To Cárdenas, the
most important person in Mexico was the schoolteacher.
Then he turned his attention to the banks, setting up special ones to furnish credit to the schools and to the new
landowners. Health programs for the people were started

and reform went ahead on every social front. When the U.S. and British oil companies refused to accept the demands of labor unions, Cárdenas took over their properties and nationalized Mexico's principal industry. No other Latin-American nation had dared do such a thing.

Perhaps the most unusual thing Cárdenas did, however, took place in 1940, when he stepped down from his office and left it to another man. He was the master of Mexico and could have ruled it longer, in one way or another, but he absolutely refused to dictate policy and returned to the life of a private citizen.

It was Cárdenas, more than any other leader, who brought to a close a stage in Mexico's development which had begun with the conquest by Spain in 1521 and lasted through the dictatorship of Díaz. He freed the poor and exploited people of Mexico from the slaving of the past. On the foundations he laid, the new and modern society, which is Mexico today, was built. The men who came after him have led the nation steadily forward.

PART IV

MEXICO, A MODERN NATION

8. The Soul of Mexico

When the great revolution began in 1910, some of the young Mexican painters and writers who had been living in Europe, unable to live under the rule of Díaz, returned home to take part in the overturning of the old order. They returned to Mexico full of the artistic ideas of Paris, where most of them had been living. In Paris, they had been painting in the impressionistic style of the times. But when they got back to Mexico they turned to the historic art forms of their country, going back to the Aztecs and Mayas. Out of these strong, characteristic patterns they created a whole new way of expressing themselves which reflected the emerging, modern Mexico.

One of the young men who came home was Diego Rivera, who soon became the artistic soul of the revolution. Born in 1886, he was fortunate in having a father who encouraged his natural talent and gave him a studio of his own when he was only ten years old. He had studied in Spain. It was the conventional work he produced there which he showed when he came home in the time of Madero. Returning to Paris while the revolution raged at home, he painted in the cubist style,

Aztec art and national pride influenced Orozco, as they did Rivera,
to produce large wall paintings telling the history of Mexico.

much influenced by Picasso. From there he went to Italy where he studied fresco painting.

Back home again in 1920, Rivera became one of the leaders in art who painted scenes of the revolution on public walls. It was bright, strong painting which celebrated the new role the worker and the peasant were now going to play in Mexican life. Rivera was the head of the Syndicate of Painters who did wall paintings on public buildings under the government's sponsorship. Among his many famous frescoes in Mexico (he also painted in the United States) are those on the National Agricultural College at Chapingo, and those which tell the story of the conquest of Mexico on the walls of the Cortés palace in Cuernavaca. In Mexico City we can see today his landscaped stairway which connects the frescoed corridors of the Ministry of Education, the frescoes showing Aztec history in the National Palace, and others in the Social Security Hospital No. 1. Rivera died in Mexico City in 1957.

Probably the greatest genius of the new movement, however, was José Clemente Orozco. He was not only a muralist but an easel painter and lithographer as well. Like Rivera, he had strong social beliefs. Born in 1883 at Ciudad Guzmán, Jalisco, he grew up in Mexico City and studied scientific agriculture at the College of Chapingo, but later went to the National University to study architecture. Tragically, he lost one hand in a chemical explosion, and began in 1909 to paint. He joined Rivera's syndicate, doing frescoes in the patio of the National Preparatory School and

After the revolution, Diego Rivera begain to paint in a new style
for his people and about his people.

at the Industrial School in Orizaba. Privately on commission he also did the main stairway of the House of Tiles in Mexico City.

Orozco's powerful style can be seen in this country at Pomona College in California, where his "Prometheus" fresco made him famous in the United States; and also in New York, where his murals decorate the New School for Social Research; and at Dartmouth College, which has his painting, "Epic of New World Culture." His work can be seen in many places in Mexico. It also hangs in several museums in the United States. The Museum of Modern Art, New York, has his painting, "Zapatistas," which tells us so well of the spirit of the revolution. Orozco died in 1949.

Another painter who caught that spirit in a grand, expressive idea was David Alfaro Siqueiros. Like Orozco, Siqueiros owed much of his inspiration to Aztec art, and drew from it a clear, forceful impression of how Mexicans lived and worked. Born in Chihuahua in 1898, he served in the constitutionalist army, and later began a career that combined art with being a propagandist for socialist causes. His vivid wall paintings, indoors and outdoors, were lacquers sprayed on with paint guns. As did Rivera and Orozco, he painted pictures which showed the great political and social changes in Mexico. In Mexico City his dazzling work can be seen in the Palace of Fine Arts, the Polytechnic Institute, the National University, and other places. Many of his paintings are in private collections in the United States and in museums.

All the forms of art were touched by the turbulence of the revolution and the awakening of a new national life which followed it. In music, the leader was Carlos Chávez, Mexico's leading composer and conductor, who was born in the capital city in 1899. When he was only nineteen, he had written his first symphony, drawing on the folk songs of Mexico for ideas but casting his work in the new, modern forms of the twentieth century. His first important work in the Mexican style was a ballet, *El fuego nuevo,* composed in 1921. Seven years later, after studying and traveling in the United States and Europe, Chávez became conductor of the Orquesta Sinfónica de México and director of the National Conservatory. Under his talented hands, the orchestra became one of the world's fine symphonic organizations and is heard often on recordings. Chávez has conducted most of the major orchestras in the United States, often in performances of his own compositions including his noted works, "Sinfonía de Antigona," "Sinfonía India," and "Sinfonía Romántica." His music is Mexican in its rhythm and melodies, but his style is individual and sophisticated.

In literature, the great novelist of the revolution was Mariano Azuela, who was born in 1873. It was Azuela who wrote of responsibility, honesty, justice, integrity, kindness, and human dignity. He made the novel in Mexico truly Mexican. His novels of the revolution showed the struggle for freedom of the "underdogs," the peasants and workers. Those he wrote later are about the results of the revolution as he saw them in his fellow Mexicans and in their country. The other major novelist of the revolution was Martín Luis Guzmán, best known for *El águila y la Serpiente*. Azuela was most interested in the "underdogs," but Guzmán searched for the revolution's causes among the "upper dogs." *El águila* tells the story of revolutionary leaders, analyzing the political plotting and scheming in detail.

Other novelists of a different kind have appeared since the revolution. Some have written about the slums and lower classes in Mexico, others about Indian life, still others about the country towns and what goes on in them. Novelists today are still working hard to write what might be called the "national novel" of Mexico.

In the drama, since 1925 there has been a steady growth, a real flowering of playwriting, centered in the National Institute of Fine Arts. Today there is a very active Mexican theater, with many new playhouses in Mexico City and great public interest in the work of Mexican playwrights.

Mexico City, the national capital, is one of the world's great cities.

9. A Changing Mexico

Most of the activity in the arts, naturally, has taken place in the cities, which have grown steadily since the end of the revolution. Like the rest of the world, Mexico is developing an urban culture too. Its cities are modern and are spreading out in all directions, as they do everywhere in these days of exploding populations. Mexico City is one of the world's great cities. Thousands of visitors from all over the world walk down its tree-lined Paseo de la Reforma, the famous commercial street, with its fine shops and hotels. Skyscrapers rise up from the city's center, expressways carry traffic over its crowded streets, and apartment buildings of every kind spring up as the city bulges outward. As in every city, there are still large slum areas, but the Mexicans have done much to build new housing for the poor on a large scale. Many government employees live in low-rent apartment developments.

There are other important cities. In the north there are the mining and manufacturing centers of Monterrey, Saltillo, Monclova, Chihuahua, Torreón, and Durango. In the south there are manufacturing and tourist centers like Guadalajara and Puebla. Veracruz and La Huasteca are oil and fishing towns on the Gulf of Mexico. Tourists fill the streets of Taxco and Acapulco on the Pacific, along with artists, painters, and writers from most of the Western world.

The people of Mexico live today in an economy that continues to change rapidly as the industrialization that began after the revolution increases year by year. In the building and owning of its own industry lies the key to Mexico's future, as every politician beginning with Calles has well understood. Since 1940, one government after another has done much to improve the standard of living among the people. This process has moved ahead even faster since the end of the Second World War. Workers produce far more today, and the per capita income of Mexicans living in cities has increased.

Now and then a slowdown occurs in the Mexican economy, but these interruptions are seen only as a reflection of the need to put more money in factories, highways, transportation, power, irrigation, health, and education. Manufacturing, once so small and unimportant a part of Mexican life, is today an important part of the economy. About 13 per cent of working Mexicans earned their living in industry by 1960, as compared with 27 per cent in the United States. The largest industry in Mexico is textiles, while the iron and steel industry is second. Assembling automobiles accounts for only a little more than 1 per cent of the work force, but it is growing. Other industries include brewing beer, making cigars and cigarettes, turning out building materials like glass and cement, making paper and pulp, and manufacturing tires and tubes for the rapidly increasing number of automobiles.

Cotton, a chief factor in the textile industry, dominates agriculture, and, along with other agricultural products, represents Mexico's chief exports. Mexico's iron and steel industry is probably the oldest in Latin America.

One way to measure a country's modernization is the size of its indoor plumbing industry, and in Mexico the manufacture of plumbing fixtures, while it is still not a large and important industry by any means, continues to grow as the cities grow. Investment by other countries in Mexico was cut down after Calles, but foreigners still own a large part of Mexican manufacturing, even though some products like motion pictures, beverages, and rubber goods are by law forced to be at least 51 per cent Mexican-owned. But investment capital from the United States and western Europe continues to pour in. Significantly, more of it goes today into manufacturing than into mining, power, and transportation, as it did in the old days.

Agriculture, however, is the solid base of the Mexican economy, as it has been for hundreds of years. The revolution may have changed its structure, but that economy still is made up of farms and ranches. Agriculture, forestry, and fishing together provide work for more than 55 per cent of the labor force.

The "five c's"—corn, cotton, cattle, coffee, and cane (meaning sugar)—are the basic products, with corn the leader because it is the staple of the Mexican diet. Mostly it is grown by the communal farmers and the private landowners, to be sold in Mexico, while cotton is a "cash crop" to be sold to other countries.

One thing the revolution was able to do was to put to death the hacienda and its feudal system of wealth

for the owner and poverty for the workers on its broad
acres of land. The haciendas are no longer important.
Replacing them are large modern farms and small, private farms operating at a level just high enough to feed
their owners and the big co-operatives which Cárdenas
brought into being when he began to redistribute the
land. Almost a third of the land under cultivation in
Mexico today is in the *ejidos,* or communal farms. The
hacienda itself has virtually disappeared. Landless farm
laborers have been resettled by the government on land
that they have been given the chance to develop.

Although it has been a slow process, the new me-
chanical methods of modern agriculture have been
introduced more and more. At the same time irrigation
projects have changed large areas of once useless land
into fertile places where the tractors chug their way
through rich crops. Mexico has come farther along the
agriculture modernization road, perhaps, than any other
Latin-American country.

What Calles and Cárdenas began in modernizing
transportation has been carried on by later governments. A staggering amount of work needed to be
done because Mexico was so far behind in this field.
But a combination of public and private ownership
in both transportation and communications has lifted
some parts of these industries rapidly in the past
twenty-five years. Other parts have grown hardly at all
and some have even grown worse. Mexican railroads,
for example, were developed in the nineteenth century, but they have grown very little for the past

The government built dams which have made it possible
to farm lands where once nothing would grow.

thirty years. This, of course, is also true of the United States. Today Mexico's fourteen railroads are government owned. They carry more freight tonnage than ever but, as in the United States, passenger travel keeps on declining as bus travel increases.

The buses travel on a modern highway system that the government has been developing since the early 1940s. There are more miles of surfaced roads in Mexico than in any other Latin-American country, yet a large percentage of Mexican highways are unpaved, and feeder roads are in extremely short supply and badly kept up. This acts as handicap for the farmers in getting their crops to the market. Other parts of the economy are cramped in the same way because of the lack of roads between different parts of the country. Nevertheless, truck transportation is one of the fastest growing businesses in Mexico. Only native-born Mexican citizens can own a trucking firm. The federal government issues franchises to the various lines, and both federal and state governments regulate them.

In spite of the competition buses have given the railroads, only about a quarter of them are engaged in long-distance hauling. The other three quarters are in local transit lines. Nevertheless, seven hundred and fifty different private firms operate six thousand buses in interstate service.

As for other forms of transportation, relatively little commerce is carried in ships in spite of Mexico's long coast line, since there are few good harbors and the land border with the United States is more important. Less than 50 per cent of exports and imports go by sea, and most of Mexico's overseas trade is carried by ships flying foreign flags.

Lack of roads, long distances, and rough land have done a great deal to increase airfreight traffic in Mexico, which uses this means of transport more than the United States does. Still, rail, truck, and water carriers handle more. Passenger traffic, however, is essential to the tourist industry, and Mexico has two major airlines for domestic and international travel, the government-controlled Aeronaves de Mexico and the private Companía Mexicana de Aviación. Pan American World Airways has a minor interest in Companía. Another line is Guest Aerovias de Mexico, 80 per cent government owned. All three of these lines have domestic routes, and there are twenty other secondary airlines for travel in the country. Several foreign flag airlines also fly to Mexico.

In the field of communications, Teléfonos de México, privately owned by Mexican interests, controls telephone facilities. There are five other private systems in various parts of the country, operating locally, and the federal government also has a few facilities of its own. Service is still inadequate, considering the number of people in the country; Mexico ranks only eighth in Latin America in the number of telephones per person. The government controls telegraph service through its Telégrafos Nacionales de México.

As in many developing countries, television is increasingly popular, but radio is more important as a means of communication, since more people have it. There are two major radio chains, with about ninety stations each, and another chain with about thirty stations, besides many independent stations.

Even so, Mexico, with ninety radio sets for every thousand people, is far behind both Argentina and Uruguay, which have two hundred per thousand. Among the first of the Latin-American nations to have commercial television, Mexico City has been transmitting programs since 1950, and there are now more than ten stations. Mexico leads most of Latin America in the use of this medium, yet in 1960 it had only eighteen sets per thousand people while Cuba boasted an average of fifty-five per thousand. The government regulates Mexican radio and television, but the stations are privately owned.

Motion pictures are the most popular form of communication in Mexico, which has more movie theaters than any other Latin-American country, besides a thriving producing center that provides films for most of the Spanish-speaking world. Newspapers are important mostly in the cities, since many people still cannot read in rural areas, but Mexico ranks second only to Argentina among Latin-American countries in the number of its papers.

It is easy to see, then, that Mexico has come a very long way since the terrible, violent days of the revolution, when it sometimes seemed that the country would be destroyed in the process of winning its freedom. There has been increasing stability since the revolution ended in 1920; there have been no uprisings since then, and since 1946 all the presidents have been civilians and not military men.

People in the United States sometimes find it hard to understand Mexico as a developing democracy. They see that it has democratic objectives, the product of the revolution, but in carrying them out it is becoming more and more a welfare state, although in the best possible way. It is also a one-party country, in any practical sense. The Institutional Revolutionary Party has little opposition. It controls the elections and, therefore, all of Mexico's legislative bodies. The Constitution says that the three branches of government are equal, but in practice the President's power and influence control everything.

In spite of all that has been done, the basic cause of Mexico's troubles remains: living standards are low and, like so many other countries, a few people have a great deal of money and most of the others have little.

But stubbornly, persistently, the government continues to press toward carrying out the promises of the Constitution, which have proved to be so hard to realize. There is a slow but constant rise in living standards as a result of government programs in industry, public works, agriculture, transportation, education, health, and sanitation. Economic stability is greater with every year. Mexicans themselves have an increasing sense of national community. Out of all this must come a working democracy.

It should be remembered that government by democracy is relatively new to Mexico. Political democracy was talked about but not practiced before the revolution in 1910, and it did not begin to happen until more than ten years after the revolution was over. Social and economic democracy were even farther away from the Mexican way of life. To be against democracy was actually a part of Mexican culture, in some respects. Consequently there has had to be change in both Mexico and the Mexicans as individuals to make democracy possible at all.

There are some high barriers remaining before it can be achieved. Geography, for example, so separates Mexicans from each other by means of mountains and deserts that it is hard for many of them to accept the idea of a nation. They tend to be interested only in their own communities, especially the Indians, who may also speak only an Indian language. It requires much better systems of transportation and communication to break down this barrier.

Again, Mexicans have had little practice in living as a democracy. For three hundred years they lived under Spanish governors and then under dictators. The idea that the individual has a right to help make government policies and to share in what the society produces is something that the leaders since the revolution have had to plant in the minds of Mexicans, who are still not quite used to it.

Another problem is the old economic one. Science and industry need to grow more. The farmers must be made to produce the extra crops needed by an urban, industrial society, yet the number of farmers raising just enough food for themselves and families with no surplus and the lack of land and water resources are a constant handicap. Illiteracy is a major problem, since democracy cannot work unless the citizens are able to read and write and therefore understand for what and whom they are voting. About 35 per cent of Mexicans have not learned to read. The nation also struggles with government employees who, because of low salaries, have become corrupt in the taking of bribes. This leads to, among other things, very little trust in public officials, who are the working apparatus of a democracy. Matters are improving, but there is still too much corruption among Mexican civil servants.

In common with other nations, Mexico faces a huge barrier to realizing democracy in its rapidly growing population. The number of people in Mexico increased by 130.4 per cent between 1910 and 1960. This means that the government must invest more and more of its money in taking care of its people, and less in the capital investments, such as factories which would result in raising living standards. National planning continues to be in the direction of industrial and agricultural growth.

But the revolution continues to go on. Stable governments, a growing economy, and sheer persistence seem likely to move Mexico closer with every year to its own ideal of democracy, which it has struggled so hard for so long to attain.

PART V

MEXICO AND THE UNITED STATES

10. The Borderlands

A close relationship between the United States and Mexico has to happen, if for no better reason than their sharing of a long, common border.

From the days of the early Spanish missions, the Southwest and California were closely related to Mexico as outlying colonies. There has been an interchange of cultures from the beginning.

But relations between Mexico and the United States have often been stormy, and have gone through three different stages. At the beginning there was a feeling of closeness when the United States encouraged Mexico to become independent and was the first to recognize it as a nation. Then came a long period when the spreading growth of the United States clashed with the stormy development of Mexico. The antagonisms and hatred stirred up during that time left hard memories on both sides. But since the 1930s, when President Franklin D. Roosevelt began his Good Neighbor Policy, relations have been increasingly better and they have never been firmer than they are today.

The road to friendship between the two countries has been a hard and rough one, however. There was a war between the two nations in the 1800s over the land which is now the state of Texas. In the 1820s, the Mexican government became worried about the United States policy of Manifest Destiny. It seemed to them that the United States thought of itself as the only nation on the North American continent destined to expand in any direction it chose. One of those directions was the Territory of Texas, which the Mexicans claimed as their own land.

To counter the U.S. move toward colonizing this area, the Mexican government began a policy which was more generous than wise. It granted Texas land to Anglo-Americans, called *empresarios*. The empresarios had to agree to parcel out this property to immigrants, at least one hundred families within the grant. All of these families had to become Mexican citizens and had to pay $30 for the square league of land they lived on. Several other special favors were offered to the empresarios. The Mexican government lowered tariff barriers for them and permitted them private police forces. Slavery was at first allowed, although in 1829 the Mexican government abolished it in all its territories.

This scheme succeeded all too well. The frontier was settled, as the Mexicans hoped, but inevitably conflicts arose between them and the Anglo-Americans. Two brothers, who were empresarios in eastern Texas, actually set up an independent Republic of Fredonia in 1826 and 1827. This rebellion was not successful, largely because of the efforts of such empresarios as

Stephen F. Austin, for whom the Texas city is named. But rebellion and war were only postponed. Austin made a trip to Mexico in the hope of stopping it, but the Texas Anglo-Americans were itching for independence. They were angry at the Mexican government for freeing their slaves, taking away their privileges, and combining Texas and Coahuila, on the border, into one state.

The war, when it came, was a short but bloody one. It began in 1835, when the Mexican President, Santa Anna, placed Texas under military rule and sent in troops to seize the custom house at Anáhuac. The colonists, in reply, captured the town garrison. Gathering up an army of four thousand men, Santa Anna marched to Texas himself. On February 24, 1836, he attacked the fortress of the Alamo, where the colonial leader William B. Travis, with 186 other men, stood ready to resist him. Santa Anna gave them the choice of surrendering, but knowing they would probably be shot by a firing squad in any case, the colonists chose to fight it out. This heroic defense, which is honored by Texans today, was brave but useless. The defenders were massacred. A month later, three hundred more Texans were killed in the same way at Goliad.

Meanwhile, Texas was organizing itself. It had declared itself an independent republic on March 2, and Austin had gone to Washington, D.C., for help. The new "nation" had an army under the command of Sam Houston. For a time, however, it looked as though the Republic of Texas was little more than a rebellious gesture, as Santa Anna's army pushed across Texas to Galveston Bay. The Mexican leader was so sure of himself that he grew careless enough to lay himself open to a surprise attack by the Texans at the San Jacinto River. Here he found himself defeated and captured. By the treaty signed on May 14, he was supposed to guarantee that Texas would be recognized as independent, but the Mexican Congress would have none of this document. Meanwhile, the clever general came back home in style on a United States warship.

Wisely, Santa Anna retired to his hacienda while another of the endless struggles for power went on in Mexico City. A junta of extremely conservative generals, backed by the Church, set up a dictatorship. Then came a succession of generals and civilians as presidents. Mexico was on the brink of chaos when the warring factions found themselves forced to unite to defend themselves against the French army and navy. France had come to collect a debt of six thousand pesos that after ten years of negotiation the Mexicans had failed to pay. The French were beaten off and the British agreed to act as a middle man and help settle the dispute.

In the end, Santa Anna gained from the power struggle. When the conservative generals finally managed to capture control of the government, it was Santa Anna they called upon to become President. After some further confusion he began to rule under a new and oppressive Constitution which ended civil liberties of every kind. It took a moderate general,

José Joaquín Herrera, to topple Santa Anna, who fled to exile in Havana, Cuba.

These events were a prelude to the war which is called the Mexican War in the United States, and, in Mexico, the War with the United States. Historians do not agree about why it started. The empresario system was partly to blame, of course. Some students of the war think it was a plot by the slaveholders, who wanted to annex Mexico, or at least part of it. Others deny this theory on the ground that slavery was forbidden by Mexican law. Mexican historians say the war was the result of Manifest Destiny—in short, imperialism. At least one U.S. historian believes rich northern Mexicans wanted the United States to conquer Mexico. They hoped the United States would bring stability and the chance to make money, while at the same time politicians found that it was popular and a guaranteed vote getter to speak out in public against the United States. There are even those who think President Polk deliberately started the war.

Whatever truth there may be in any of these ideas, it was a fact that, since diplomacy had failed and the Mexican government had refused to recognize Texan independence, there was little choice but war, inasmuch as the United States evidently meant to annex Texas. Only the year before, in 1845, a special U.S. agent, John Slidell, had approached the Mexicans with a proposition that they recognize the Río Grande as the boundary. In return for this, they would receive twenty-five million dollars which would pay for California and the land northwest of El Paso. If this did not work, Slidell had the authority to buy New Mexico for five million dollars. But Mexican politicians dared not sell, although they needed the money desperately. To sell so much Mexican soil to the United States would be political suicide.

General Herrera told Slidell politely that diplomatic relations with the United States could not be re-established under the circumstances. He was willing to talk over the question of Texas, but unwilling to sell anything. Even talking to Slidell was enough to cost Herrera his job. His rivals charged that he was listening to the U.S. offers and was paying no attention to the far more important problem of Texas. He had to resign, and Slidell was handed his passport and sent home on March 21, 1846.

A few days later, General Zachary Taylor was facing the Mexicans across the Río Grande, at Matamoros, in what Mexicans claimed was Mexican territory. He refused to withdraw when the Mexicans asked him to, and on April 25, a clash came between Mexican cavalry and U.S. dragoons, in which several of the U.S. mounted horsemen were killed. That was enough to make President Polk ask Congress for a declaration of war. May 21, the United States declared war.

It was not a popular war in the United States. Antislavery people in the North and East thought of it as another move on the part of Southern slaveholders to extend slavery. Nor were the Mexicans entirely enthusiastic about the prospect of war. The politicians could make capital out of it, but the poor, demoralized

The Mexican-American War was one of the most unpopular wars ever fought by the United States and was given very little support.

masses, already struggling against a chaotic dictatorship, saw the war with so powerful a neighbor as a new disaster.

General Mariano Arista's troops fought bravely and well in several battles along the Río Grande, but they were outmaneuvered at last and had to retreat to Matamoros, which Taylor soon captured on his drive toward Monterrey. That city fell to him on September 25, after a hard struggle along the way.

Other U.S. troops began to move. Colonel Stephen W. Kearny's frontiersmen marched from Fort Leavenworth to Santa Fe, which he entered on August 16 with little trouble. He promptly claimed New Mexico for the United States. Kearny then split up his force and marched part of it to California, where he found that territory (it was called Upper California then) already in U.S. hands for the most part. There were few settlers there and they were divided in their loyalties. California fell with hardly a struggle by January 1847.

Taylor's army meanwhile plunged on south of the Río Grande and joined General John E. Wool's San Antonio expedition near Buena Vista, Mexico. Santa Anna was on his way from San Luis Potosí to confront him with a strong army, but Taylor did not know it. He obeyed an order from his superior, General Winfield Scott, to send most of his troops to him for an attack on Mexico City. As a result, Taylor was left with only five thousand men to face Santa Anna's fifteen thousand at Buena Vista. It was not a brilliant military engagement by any means. Both commanders made serious mistakes and lost an unnecessary number of men. Finally Santa Anna withdrew under cover of night, retreating back toward San Luis Potosí. He could not match U.S. artillery and bayonets. And now, somehow, he had to get his hungry army through the winter.

The war in northern Mexico ended soon after, and the scene of battle shifted to the country's vital supply route from Veracruz to Mexico City. For seven months the struggle went on for central Mexico. With thirteen thousand men and the help of the Navy, Scott captured Veracruz in March 1847. But Santa Anna marshaled an army of twelve thousand soldiers and met Scott on April 17 and 18 at Cerro Gordo, where he defeated the Mexicans in a battle that sent them reeling back in retreat to Puebla and then to Mexico City. Scott could have ended the war at that point, but he had to wait three months in Puebla for more men and supplies. That gave Santa Anna the chance to raise the strength of his army to twenty-five thousand and to fortify the approaches to the capital. With a force numbering somewhat less than eleven thousand, Scott approached Mexico City on August 7, and in a series of bloody battles—all the bloodier because the Mexican artillery was manned in part by expert U.S. artillerymen who had deserted—he pushed Santa Anna slowly backward.

The Mexicans fought with skill and great bravery. At the battle for Chapultepec, some of the young Mexican cadets committed suicide rather than surrender to Scott's superior force. Santa Anna himself tried every device he could think of, including an armistice called to negotiate peace during which he regrouped his forces. The stubborn old general refused to give up. He led a last, desperate, futile charge against a small detachment of U.S. soldiers at Puebla, after which he had to flee for his life to the mountains, where he planned to carry on guerrilla warfare.

Such warfare might have been possible if Mexico had been united, but the nation was in a state of confusion. Yucatán was in rebellion. The northern states were about to secede. A moderate peace party in the capital held what national power there was, and these men were ready to try to end the struggle. Santa Anna had no choice but to give up his guerrilla campaign. In the tradition of the day he sat down with U.S. officers at a banquet as soon as peace was established, after which he was sent off to the island of Jamaica in exile. By July 1848 the last of Scott's army had sailed away from Veracruz. The war was over.

As a matter of fact, the two nations had been trying to find their way toward a peace treaty for over a year. In April 1847 Nicholas P. Trist, the Department of State's chief clerk, had arrived in Mexico as a secret agent. He had been sent by James Buchanan, the Secretary of State, with power to conclude a treaty whenever it was possible. Trist had to deal with Scott, however, and the general, who was known with good reason as "Old Fuss and Feathers," was not about to give away any of his power as field commander. Scott believed those powers included the right to negotiate peace. It was not surprising, therefore, that he quarreled violently with Trist, and it took considerable pressure from Washington to convince both men that they must work together.

While he was still President, Santa Anna had refused to have peace talks with the United States and especially with Trist. He thought that the U. S. Government had insulted Mexico by sending only a chief clerk as its emissary. The Mexican Congress sided with him for a time, but as Scott continued his victorious march, they began to waver, and after Santa Anna's defeat at Puebla, the moderates gained control. Manuel de la Peña y Peña took over the presidency from Santa Anna and began to negotiate with Trist, who unfortunately found himself without the authority to carry on because President Polk, responding to political pressures, had recalled him. Nevertheless, the chief clerk, an arrogant man, decided to ignore his recall orders and continue the negotiations.

At last a treaty of "peace, friendship, limits, and settlement" was signed between the two nations on February 2, 1848, at Guadalupe Hidalgo. In it, Trist had carried out his original instructions from Secretary Buchanan. He succeeded in gaining the cession from Mexico of more than half of its land. Mexico also agreed to give up Texas. In return, the United States was to pay Mexico fifteen million dollars, certainly a small price for the great area of land from west Texas to the Pacific Coast. The treaty also canceled all claims against Mexico by U.S. citizens, but these claims were limited to three and a quarter million dollars.

This treaty did not pass the United States Senate without a hot debate, which revolved mainly around the question of slavery. Southern senators thought the boundary had been set too far north. Northern senators, on the other hand, thought the South was getting far more territory than it deserved, but none of them wanted to give any land back to Mexico. In the end, the treaty passed by a narrow vote and came into force on July 4, 1848.

There was much unhappiness with the treaty among many highly placed Mexicans, as well, and it was no sooner signed than further arguments arose between the two countries. There were differences of opinion about the boundary, which in fact had been drawn contrary to geographic facts. There were arguments, too, about the rights given to each nation to build a road, canal, or railway within a marine mile from either side of the Gila River and about the responsibility of the United States Government to do something about stopping Indian raids into Mexican territory. At the bottom of the quarrels was the desire of the U.S. expansionists to stretch the influence and possessions of the United States as far as possible.

In 1852, with a new U. S. President in power, Franklin Pierce, and with Santa Anna back from exile and once more in the saddle as President of Mexico, the time seemed to have come for renegotiations, par-

ticularly because Santa Anna's government desperately
needed money. The U.S. commissioner this time was
General James Gadsden, who, in his lifetime, had risen
from soldier to railroad president. He began his work
in Mexico City in August 1853, meeting with Foreign
Minister Manuel Díaz de Bonilla. After four months of
talks, an agreement was reached: Mexico agreed to
sell some more land south of the Gila River, which
would benefit the U.S. railroaders who wanted to build
a transcontinental line through it. The United States
gained about nineteen million acres for fifteen million
dollars, later reduced to ten million dollars by the U. S.
Senate. This deal is known in U.S. history as the Gadsden
Purchase. It was ratified on May 31, 1854, by Mexico,
and on June 29 by the United States.

11. "The Colossus of the North"

The Gadsden Purchase was not the last land that a Mexican government, badly in need of cash, would consider selling for U.S. dollars. Facing bankruptcy in 1858, the Juárez government negotiated a treaty with the United States which would have traded another large slice of territory for four million dollars, but neither the U. S. Senate nor the Mexican liberals would approve it.

Money, or the lack of it, was a basic difficulty in Mexico's foreign policy. It was the Mexican Congress' decision in 1861 to delay the payments on its debts to foreign countries that led to France, England, and Spain to decide to use military force and collect their money at gunpoint. The United States made no move to stop this unwise move, except to tell the Spanish government that intervention must not destroy the republican form of government in Mexico or lead to territorial conquest. But the U.S., caught up in its own terrible Civil War, did not interfere when France, carrying on alone after Britain and Spain withdrew, set up the preposterous Maximilian I as Emperor.

The Civil War in the United States ended, however, while the French army was still in Mexico setting up

Maximilian's regime. On February 12, 1866, the United States took notice of the Mexican situation by demanding that France withdraw her troops. It came as no surprise to the French. They were well aware of the United States' strong feelings against the whole undertaking, but had counted on her to be too busy with her own affairs to do anything. Now, faced with stronger opposition, and threatened by the Prussians at home, the French government wisely withdrew its forces, leaving Maximilian to fend for himself, with the tragic results already discussed.

With the Emperor gone and Juárez back in power, the United States made a special effort to help the Mexican government restore itself. Secretary of State Seward himself made a trip to Mexico City in 1869, bringing his government's expressions of friendship. Juárez welcomed him, but his opposition did not. The Mexican War was not so easily forgotten, nor could Seward so quickly live down his record as an expansionist and believer in Manifest Destiny.

Yet those who were against Juárez on these grounds were no better off when the stubborn old leader died in 1872 and his once faithful general, Porfirio Díaz, who had come to lead the opposition, became President in 1876. Díaz became the president who opened the door wide to foreign land barons and investors, mainly the United States. He saved his country economically but sacrificed its revolutionary ideals under the iron hand of his dictatorship.

The United States did not recognize Díaz when he

first became President because it was not certain how he would deal with several unsettled questions between the two nations. An agreement settling U.S. claims had been signed in 1868, for example, but no one knew whether Díaz would honor it. It was not known, either, whether he would take a strong hand in putting down the bandits and cattle rustlers who were bothering U.S. citizens along the border.

Fortunately, Díaz had an extraordinary secretary of foreign relations, Ignacio Luis Vallarta. Vallarta reassured the United States on all the disputed points and succeeded in gaining full recognition for the government in May 1878.

After this came the flood of U.S. investment. Most of Mexico's three billion pesos of foreign investment came from across the border. Much of it went into the development of gold, silver, and copper mining, and oil. It was this kind of takeover of Mexican resources, at the expense of its citizens, particularly the workers and peasants, as well as the many injustices of the Díaz regime, which led to the revolution of 1910–20.

Oddly enough, the United States gave shelter to some of the revolutionaries who were trying to overthrow Díaz, particularly the Flores Magón brothers, Ricardo, Enrique, and Jesús. They set up their headquarters in St. Louis in 1905, after fleeing from Mexico. There they published their journal, *La Regeneración.* This publication made Díaz so angry that he sued the Magones for libel in U.S. court and had them arrested. But the Magones survived, got their paper into print again, and on July 1, 1906, published in St. Louis their famous *Programa del Partido Liberal,* which was a blueprint for overthrowing Díaz.

The Magones were not the only sources of Díaz' troubles. A strike in 1906 at a U.S.-owned copper mine in Sonora was put down ruthlessly by government troops and Americans with guns. This led to the wide belief that Díaz was pro-American, an idea no one could reasonably doubt in any case. There were other bloody strikes, many of them inspired by the *Magonistas,* and all put down by government soldiers, thus further stirring up the hatred of labor.

It was not all clear sailing for the Magonistas who lived in the United States and directed revolutionary activities from there. One of them, Ricardo Flores Magón, was arrested for violation of the Espionage Act and was sentenced to twenty years in Leavenworth Prison, where he died in 1922.

In a way he could not foresee, Díaz had also made a mistake in tying his fortunes too closely to the U.S. economy. When a severe business slump struck the United States in 1907, its backwash nearly drowned Mexico's prosperity. This was followed two years later by disastrous crop failures, which sowed the seeds of rebellion among Mexico's starving peasants.

When the revolution finally broke out in 1910, Díaz found himself without the support of Washington. This was partly because of his own greed and stupidity in dealing with British oil interests at the expense of those in the United States. The United States sent troops down to the border supposedly to protect U.S. interests, but Díaz was afraid it might mean armed intervention. He pleaded with Washington not to stop the revolutionaries passing back and forth freely across the border, and the United States agreed, but it was already too late. Madero, the revolution's first leader, had returned.

But Madero did not have the support of the United States when he finally came to power, and it was the U. S. Ambassador to Mexico City, Henry Lane Wilson, who helped to bring him down. Wilson plotted with the opposing army generals to make General Victoriano Huerta the temporary President until Díaz could succeed him at the next elections. After Madero and his vice-president, Pino Suárez, had been arrested, Wilson told of this agreement with the generals in front of foreign diplomats at the United States Embassy. The other diplomats then signed the document, which was called the Pact of the Embassy.

To the ambassador's amazement, his government accepted neither the agreement nor his recommendation that Huerta's government be recognized at once. President Woodrow Wilson was about to take office. It was believed that he would not approve of the existence of any government which had seized power by force, as Huerta's had done. His resistance was virtually guaranteed when Madero and Suárez were murdered on their way to prison.

For a time Huerta was not so badly off as the U. S. President's refusal to accept him might have forecast. Great Britain, the European powers, China, and Japan all recognized him. English brokers came to his economic rescue with a bond issue of seven million pesos. Only the United States refused recognition. Henry Wilson was recalled. President Wilson not only refused recognition or aid, but also sent an agent to Mexico with a request that Huerta resign and a new election be held. After that, he said, the United States would consider a loan. Naturally, Huerta had no idea of giving up his office, and instead persuaded the Mexican Congress to demand that he stay. Wilson's reponse was to lift an embargo on arms shipments to Mexico. This opened the way to supplying Huerta's enemies with the tools they needed for his destruction.

This action insured the success of Carranza's Army of the Constitution, Huerta's chief opposition, which had won control of northern Mexico by April 1914. President Wilson made a further move planned to overthrow Huerta when he intervened at Tampico, Mexico, where some U.S. sailors had been arrested by federal troops. Although they were quickly released, their commanding admiral demanded that the Mexicans salute the U.S. flag with twenty-one guns. Mexico refused to do so, and the U.S. troops then seized the port of Veracruz, not so much to put pressure on the Mexican government, but to prevent a shipment of munitions from being delivered to Huerta.

At Veracruz, Mexican and U.S. troops fought each other, and about two hundred of Huerta's soldiers were killed. All of Mexico was furious at the United States. Even Carranza, who had asked for and needed

U.S. support, was forced to denounce the seizure of the important city at the loss of so many Mexican lives. The United States was held up by Huerta as "the colossus of the north," responsible for direct intervention in Mexican affairs, as indeed was the case.

All this could not save Huerta, however. Carranza and his brilliant general overthrew him, and he escaped first to Europe, then to the United States, the country against which he had preached so loudly. There, in Texas, he attempted to hatch a new plot that would bring him back to power, but he was discovered and arrested, and soon died.

Carranza's government was recognized by the United States in October 1915. Less than five years later, he was out of power and assassinated as he tried to follow the familiar escape route for Mexican leaders, the train line from Mexico City to Veracruz. That event really ended the ten-year revolution, and a period of reconstruction began—slow, halting, and generally discouraging until Lázaro Cárdenas became President in 1934.

12. The Good Neighbor Policy

Obregón, who was elected President in 1920, had carried on his war against the Church to the point where U.S. intervention once more seemed possible. The Catholics in the United States brought pressure to bear to stop the "attack on religion" and restore whatever rights the Church had lost. Mixed in with this righteous indignation was a fear that the Mexican government might also take over the valuable properties of the U.S. oil companies.

President Warren G. Harding was now in the White House. He refused to recognize Obregón's regime until the Mexican chief assured him that the new Constitution would not be applied to U.S. oil properties, thus preventing their being taken over by the government. Even then Harding would not take Obregón's word for it, but sent commissioners to Mexico City to talk further with him. These commissioners signed the Bucareli agreements, as they were called, which not only guaranteed the protection Obregón had already promised, but provided for a claims commissions to be set up in the future to settle any later disputes. Recognition was granted at last in August 1923.

In return, when his Minister of Finance, Adolfo de la

Huerta, tried to unseat him during the following December, Obregón was able to put down this brush-fire rebellion with the help of arms from the United States. And again, as so often before, the United States gave protection to the very enemies it had helped to put down. De la Huerta escaped to Los Angeles, where he became a music teacher.

Obregón's successor in the ten years between 1924 to 1934 was Plutarco Calles, who set up what was in effect another dictatorship, with which the weary Mexicans were all too familiar. Like Obregón, he began to war against the Church when its bishops revolted against what they thought were the too liberal ideas of the new Constitution and advised their followers not to support it. This occurred in 1926, and it was followed by what amounted to a civil war between Church and state in which there was looting and burning of Catholic churches and the homes of the faithful. The faithful in turn raided the property of the government's supporters and killed a good many of them in the bargain.

During the three years of this conflict, the United States became increasingly angry about what was happening in Mexico. Senators, congressmen, and editors spoke out strongly against the struggle, and the Secretary of State, Frank B. Kellogg, joined them. But again it was not so much the attack on religion which so upset the United States as it was the fear that Calles would do what Obregón had not done for the sake of holding on to U.S. support, and that was take over the

After British and U.S. oil companies refused to pay higher wages or offer better living conditions for its workers, the Mexican government stepped in and took control of the oil companies.

oil companies' property. Calles was accused by these companies and by the Hearst newspapers, which supported them, of not keeping his promises. Under this kind of pressure, relations between the two countries grew steadily worse until the U. S. Secretary of State Kellogg could bluntly say: "The Mexican government is on trial before the world."

"All nations are always on trial before the world," Calles answered sharply, which was simple truth. It only further angered Kellogg, however, who announced that he had become convinced there was a Communist plot at work in Mexico. That charge was too much even for conservative editors and businessmen, or at least those who knew anything about Mexican history, which, as they pointed out, Kellogg did not.

An open break was avoided when Calles politely suggested that the argument be referred to the Hague International Court of Justice. U.S. businessmen said they would prefer negotiation between the two countries alone. As it happened, neither course was taken because a new President came to the White House following Harding's death and Calvin Coolidge had the good sense to appoint Dwight W. Morrow as ambassador to Mexico—the best man the United States had ever sent to represent it. Morrow was thoroughly liked and respected by the Mexican government and people. He listened to the government and the government listened to him. It was not long before the talk of the United States getting involved in Mexico ended.

When Cárdenas, the next President, came to power,

he surprised Calles by being a strong leader instead of the willing servant the ex-President intended him to be. He also surprised the United States, which expected him to carry on the former regime's policy of encouraging foreign exploitation of Mexico's resources.

As we have seen, Cárdenas was a strong friend of labor and of the peasants. Once his great land distribution program got under way, and the workers' unions grew much stronger, there was bound to be a clash with foreign interests, mainly with the United States. The crisis came in March 1938, when Cárdenas took possession of the properties of seventeen U.S. and British oil companies. He had good reason to do so. The oil workers were very badly housed and badly paid, even though their demands for higher wages and better living conditions had been upheld legally by the Mexican labor board. The companies did nothing to carry out these decisions, and the workers already had been out on strike for ten months before the government stepped in and took over.

A bitter struggle followed. Cárdenas pointed out the fact that Mexicans had owned their own subsoil since colonial days, and pointed to his nation's sovereign rights and its present views on property as belonging to the community. The oil companies answered by bringing pressure to bear on their governments to do something about the stubborn Mexicans, and in turn the governments sent strong protest notes. Cárdenas stood firm, promising only to pay the companies for the loss of their properties, using tax receipts as the basis of payment. The companies then challenged the accuracy of the receipts.

Serious trouble might have resulted, as it had in President Wilson's administration, if the war in Europe and the question of U.S. intervention had not distracted the United States. Then, too, Cárdenas was more fortunate than those before him in having a different kind of man in the White House. Franklin D. Roosevelt was the first U. S. President to do something truly constructive about Latin-American relations. His Good Neighbor Policy, whatever its weak points may have been, had an immediate good result in April 1942. It was then that a Mexican-American commission drew up a settlement of the oil claims by which the U.S. companies were paid about twenty-four million dollars. The British got twenty-one million dollars a few years later. This was far from satisfactory to the companies in either country, but they had no other choice than to accept it. As for the Mexicans, they saw the settlement as the start of their economic independence.

Since 1940, the growing industrialism in Mexico has brought our two nations closer together. The Second World War helped, too, since Mexico came to the support of the United States immediately after Pearl Harbor. President Avila Camacho and his government declared war on Germany, Italy, and Japan in May 1942. To relieve the labor shortage in the United States, an arrangement was made to send two hundred thousand Mexican migrant workers northward, and on the war front itself, three hundred Mexican pilots went to Formosa and the Philippines. As the war went on, Mexican production of copper, steel, mercury, and similar strategic materials became highly important in helping the Allies fight the war. At the end of the conflict, these war-developed industries became an equally important part of the new Mexican economy.

Even then, however, the traditional suspicion of the *norteamericanos* did not die in Mexico. It kept up all during the war in the speeches of fanatical extremists who preached that the country was being destroyed by its rulers who were in league with the United States. After the war, when Ezequiel Padilla, a strong supporter of U.S. policies, seemed to many to be the logical candidate for president to succeed Avila Camacho, it was just this support that kept Padilla from even becoming a candidate and resulted in the election of Miguel Alemán.

But Alemán proved to be a good neighbor too. He welcomed Harry S. Truman when the President flew to Mexico City to visit him. The people themselves seemed no less friendly. Later Alemán returned the visit in Washington and also made a short tour of the country. Everywhere he was greeted with enthusiasm. These friendly relations continued. Mexico got large loans from the Export-Import Bank and other United States agencies, and these were a good deal of help in aiding both industry and agriculture. Most impressive were the power projects on the east and west coasts, built with the help of U.S. capital, both private and public. This came to be known as Mexico's TVA, after the tremendous U.S. development in the Tennessee Valley. U.S. money also helped Mexico to control ,its severe problems of hoof-and-mouth disease, failing railroads, and not enough crops.

Since Alemán's day, relations between the United States and Mexico have continued to be warm and mutually helpful. It was a mark of Mexico's emergence as a full participant in the affairs of the Western Hemisphere nations when President John F. Kennedy and Mrs. Kennedy visited President López Mateos in Mexico City soon after the beloved U.S. leader entered the White House. During his regime, Mateos was able to settle an old boundary dispute with the United States and to come to an agreement about how Colorado River water should be distributed.

On other matters, however, López Mateos stood firm on issues where Mexico held a differing point of view. He would not, for example, join the United States in comdemning Fidel Castro; not getting involved in other countries' affairs was the keystone of Mexican foreign policy, as it had always been. There was no strain on the ties between the nations as a result of this difference.

President Díaz Ordaz, elected in 1964, has carried on the policies of those before him, and relations between the United States and Mexico have never been closer than they are today. We know each other better now, as tourists travel freely in both countries and

Mexican history is studied in U.S. schools and colleges. The two nations have become increasingly each other's good customer, and certainly the sale of U.S. products south of the border has been an important factor in building the affluent society of the United States.

Mexico itself still has problems and they are the same old problems. Land distribution goes ahead, but there is less and less land available to give to the people— land, that is, on which crops can be grown. The things that the revolution promised are still being carried out, but sometimes with agonizing slowness. The United States has at times done much to help fulfill those promises and will surely do more, while respecting the right and the ability of Mexicans to work out their own destiny.

On both sides of the border now there is respect and friendship for the most part, no matter what differences may occur from time to time. These good neighbors have learned to live together, as all nations must do if they are to live in a better world tomorrow.

INDEX

Agriculture (farming), 8ff., 34, 82ff.
Airplanes, 87
Alvarez, Juan, 41
Anáhuac, 94. *See also* Valley of Anáhuac
Anza, Juan Bautista de, 3
Architecture, 35
Arista, Mariano, 99
Arizona, 3, 4, 6, 12
Arts, the, 35, 73–79
Austin, Stephen F., 94
Automobiles, 82
Aztecs, 18, 21–24, 25ff., 29, 33, 73ff.
Azuela, Mariano, 65, 78–79

Britain (England), 42, 95, 105, 108–10;
   oil companies, 72, 107, 114, 116
Bucareli agreements, 112
Buchanan, James, 101, 102
Buena Vista, 99–100
Buses, 86

California, 3ff., 9, 10, 12, 33, 77, 92, 96, 99
Calles, Plutarco, 68, 69–71, 113–16
Cárdenas, Lázaro, 67–68, 69–72, 111, 115–16
Carlotta, Empress, 43
Carranza, Venustiano, 57–58, 59, 62, 66, 110–11
Celaya, 59
Cerro Gordo, 100
Chalco, 29
Chapultepec, 100
Chávez, Carlos, 78
Chiapas, 17, 20
Chichén Itzá, 21
Chihuahua, 57, 62, 81
Church, the (Christianity), 29, 30, 34–35, 37–38, 42, 95, 112, 113; missions, vi, 3, 4
Churches and cathedrals, 32, 35, 38–40
Ciudad Juárez, 55
Coahuila, 94
Colorado, 12
Columbus, New Mexico, 59
Communications, 87–88
Coolidge, Calvin, 115
Cortez (Cortés), Hernando, 27–33, 75
Cotton, 82–83
Creoles, 34, 37, 44, 48
Cuisine, 14

Dams, 85
Díaz, Carmen Rubio, 47, 49
Díaz, Porfirio, 44, 45–50, 51ff., 73, 106–9
Díaz de Bonilla, Manuel, 104
Díaz Ordaz, President, 119
Durango, 81

Economy, 82–84, 90–91. *See also* Labor;

specific areas, leaders
Education (schools), 5, 13, 34–35, 71
El Paso, 3, 57, 97
Empresarios, 93

Fierro, Rodolfo, 57
Flores Magón brothers, 107–8
France and the French, 42–43, 47, 95, 105–6

Gadsden Purchase, 104
Gila River, 103, 104
Goliad, 4, 94
Grijalva, Juan de, 27
Guadalajara, 81
Guadalupe Hidalgo, 102–3
Guatemala, 20, 25
Guzmán, Martín Luis, 79

Haciendas, 34, 83–84. *See also* Land
Harding, Warren G., 112, 115
Herrera, José Joaquín, 96, 97
Hidalgo, Miguel, 36, 37
Houston, Sam, 94
Huerta, Adolfo de la, 112–13
Huerta, Victoriano, 54, 57, 58, 65, 68, 109–11

Indians, 1ff., 12, 16–34, 37, 48, 63, 66, 90, 103. *See also* specific groups, persons, places
Investment, 83, 107
Iron and steel, 82, 83
Iturbide, D. Agustín de, 38–40
Ixtapalapa, 29

Juárez, Benito, 40–41ff., 105, 106

Kearny, Stephen W., 99
Kellogg, Frank B., 113, 115
Kino, Eusebio Francisco, 3

Labor, 8–9, 11, 14–15. *See also* Economy; specific fields
La Huasteca, 81
Land, 65, 66, 70–71. *See also* Agriculture
Language, 1, 12–13
Lerdo de Tejada, Sebastian, 44ff.
Limantour, José Yves, 48–49, 51
Literature (books), 35, 78–79
Los Angeles, 4, 10, 11, 113

Madero, Francisco, 51–52, 53, 55, 63, 65, 68, 109
Manufacturing, 82, 83
Matamoros, 97, 99
Maximilian I, 43, 45, 105–6
Mayapán, 21
Mayas, 16, 17, 19, 20–21, 25, 27
Mestizos, 34, 37, 44, 48